Primitive Quakerism REVIVED

Living as Friends in the Twenty-First Century

Paul Buckley

Inner Light Books
San Francisco, California

Primitive Quakerism Revived:
Living as Friends in the Twenty-First Century
© Paul Buckley, 2018
All Rights Reserved

Except for brief quotations, no part of this publication may be reproduced, stored in a retrieval system, or transmitted, in any form or by any means, electronic, mechanical, photocopy, recorded, or otherwise, without prior written permission.

Cover and book design: Paul Buckley
Rear cover photograph: Charles Moore
Editor: Charles Martin
Copy editor: Kathy McKay

Published by Inner Light Books, San Francisco, California
www.innerlightbooks.com
editor@innerlightbooks.com

Library of Congress Control Number: 2018931354

ISBN 978-0-9998332-2-3 (hardcover)
ISBN 978-0-9998332-3-0 (paperback)

And I did as truly believe that the Lord would Redeem a People out of the World, and its Ways, and Customs, Language, Marriage and Burying, and all the World's Hypocrisie; I looked for this Change, before I saw any appearance of it; but all my fear was I should not live to see it; the Enemy always following of me with his Temptations, to work me into unbelief, and to cast me down into desperation.

Elizabeth Stirredge[1]

Contents

Index of Persons Quoted — xi

Acknowledgments — xiii

Introduction — 1

  Background — 2

  Ten Signs We Need a Revival — 4

    1. God Is Not the Center of Our Lives and Our Meetings — 4

    2. Being Quaker Is Not Our Primary Identification — 4

    3. The Spread of Individualism among Friends — 5

    4. The Redefinition of Community — 5

    5. Being Unwilling to Say What We Believe — 5

    6. Ritualizing Meeting for Worship — 6

    7. Encrusting Outward Characteristics — 8

    8. Treating Outreach as an Activity — 8

    9. Accommodating to the Surrounding Culture — 9

    10. Being Admired — 10

  Disclosures — 10

    1. There Is a God — 10

    2. I Am a Christian — 11

    3. I Am a Quaker — 13

    4. God Communicates Directly with Each Person — 14

    5. Friends Have a Calling as a People — 14

6. The Society of Friends Exists Because We Serve God	15
7. Traditions Are Inevitable	15
8. People Embellish	17

Chapter 1 Quaker Revival — 19

Two Types of Revival	21
Utopian Revival	21
Radical Revival	23
The Nature of Revival among Friends	24

Chapter 2 In the Beginning — 27

George Fox	28
Robert Barclay	33
William Penn	35
The Inward Light	38
Worship in Spirit and in Truth	39
The Marks of a True Christian	40
Some Essential Concepts	41
The God or Spirit of the World	42
The Lamb's War	43
Buying and Selling in the Seventeenth Century	45
The Kingdom of Heaven on Earth	46
Salvation	48
Perfection	50

Chapter 3 Changes in Quaker Faith and Practice over Time — 53

The Light	53
The Inward Light of Christ in the Seventeenth Century	53

Contents

Searching and Revealing	54
Directing and Guiding	55
Forgiving and Empowering	55
Knowing God	56
The Analogy to Natural Light	57
The Analogy Today	59
From Inward to Inner	61
The Inner Light in the Twenty-First Century	61
Quaker Christianity	63
Quaker Christianity in the Seventeenth Century	63
The Orthodoxy of Early Quaker Beliefs	64
Why Were Friends Persecuted?	64
The One True Church	67
Quaker Christianity in the Twenty-First Century	68
Meeting for Worship	70
Worship in the Seventeenth Century	70
Changes over the Centuries	72
Worship in the Twenty-First Century	75
Speech	76
Quaker Speech in the Seventeenth Century	77
Honors and Flattery	77
Names for Days and Months	79
Greetings and Salutations	79
Oaths	80
Radical Truthfulness	80
A Mid-Course Correction	81
Quaker Speech Today	82

Reclaiming Our Heritage	82
Avoiding Discomfort	83
Inconsistencies	84
New Traditions	85
Relations with Earthly Governments	86
In the Seventeenth Century	88
Changes over the Centuries	89
French and Indian War	89
Abolition	91
American Civil War	91
Political Action among Twenty-First-Century Friends	91
Quaker Testimonies	93
Personal Testimony	94
Our Corporate Testimonies	95
The Evolution of a Quaker Witness: The Testimony against War	97
SPICES	100
Traveling in the Ministry	101

Chapter 4 How Primitive Quakerism Revived Would Look — 105

Putting God at the Center	106
Being in the World but Not of the World	108
Community	109
Community as Testimony	110
Outreach	111
Mutual Accountability and Love	115
Membership	117

Contents

The Origins of Membership	117
Membership in the Twenty-First Century	118
Meeting for Worship	120
A Worshipping Community	121
Preparation for Worship	122
Practice	123
Prayer	125
Joy	127
Why So Glum?	127
Love	129
Quaker Optimism	130
Two Essential Elements of the Quaker Way	131
Chapter 5 Being Leaven	**133**
Twelve Simple Queries	**137**
Notes	**139**

Index of Persons Quoted

Allen, William	17	Hicks, Elias	9
Anonymous	35	Howgill, Francis	121
Barclay, Robert	33, 66	Kang'ahi, Gladys	4, 110
Barrawe, Robert	131	Kelly, Thomas	106, 107, 127
Benezet, Anthony	46	Morrison, Peggy Senger	125
Besse, Joseph	101	Mott, Lucretia	129, 130
Blackborow, Sarah	11	Nayler, James	16, 43
Bownas, Samuel	123	Penington, Isaac	63, 71, 109
Branson, Ann	105	Penn, William	29, 39, 45, 53, 64, 67, 77, 114, 118
Burnyeat, John	40	Phipps, Joseph	93
Cheevers, Sarah	91	Punshon, John	133
Comstock, Elizabeth	108	Saunders, Deborah	96
Docwra, Ann	55	Scott, Job	56
Fell, Margaret	24, 50, 53, 97, 128	Stephen, Caroline	19
Fox, George	15, 29, 47, 54, 56, 57, 59, 63, 65, 98	Stirredge, Elizabeth	iii
		White, Dorothy	48
Gardner, Sunderland	117	Wilson, Louise	100
Gurney, Joseph John	14	Woolman, John	42, 87, 115

Acknowledgments

In the course of writing this book, I have had two serious bouts with cancer. At times, the treatments have left me physically and mentally weak—sometimes unable to even read. I would not have survived without the constant love and care of my wife, Peggy Spohr; without her, this book would never have been written.

During one particularly demanding period, my son, Conn Buckley, stayed with us to help Peggy. She has also had help from her sister, Carol Huster, and numerous individuals from Community and Eastern Hills Friends Meetings in Cincinnati. I am also gratefully aware of the cloud of Quakers and others who called on the phone, brought over meals, mailed me cards and notes, emailed poems and cartoons, wrapped us in love, and held us in prayer during those long months.

Robert Garris was instrumental in shaping my sense of what it means to be a loving and welcoming Quaker. Bob and I had many opportunities to work together thirty years ago when I was the presiding clerk of Illinois Yearly Meeting and he was the general superintendent of Western Yearly Meeting. The time I spent with Bob prepared me for my work as a Quaker writer.

The seeds for this book were planted almost twenty years ago when I first read William Penn's *Primitive Christianity Revived* as a student at the Earlham School of Religion. I found Penn's thinking convincing and penetrating but his writing nearly impenetrable. That inspired me to translate five of his theological works into modern English. These were published by the Earlham School of Religion Publications as *Twenty-First Century Penn* in 2003. With their permission, an updated second edition of *Primitive Christianity Revived* is being published by Inner Light Books as a companion to this volume.* Penn's book was written in a trying time for Friends, and it inspired me to write this one. It is the model I am trying to follow.

My three years at Earlham School of Religion changed my life. What was intended to be a short break from "the real world" transformed me and changed the direction of my career. I took every class that John Punshon offered and discovered a depth in Quaker thought and its scriptural roots that I had not ever imagined.

Earlham School of Religion also helped me in preparing this book and serves all Friends by hosting the Digital Quaker Collection (http://esr.earlham.edu/dqc/). Nearly all the works I have referenced are available online both as page images and searchable text versions.

Soon after, Doug Gwyn moved to Richmond, Indiana, to serve as the pastor at First Friends Meeting. Doug and I began having lunch on a regular basis, and our conversations are a second major inspiration for this work. It took me years and many more conversations to gather my thoughts together into a rough draft. Doug's review of a couple of the early chapters were critical to further sharpening my thinking.

Two events helped to pull my still-scattered reflections together. In early 2016, Cincinnati Friends Meeting was between pastors and asked me to serve them in the interim. The weekly

---

* Copies are available from Inner Light Books (www.innerlightbooks.com).

Acknowledgments

work of preparing a message that would speak to their needs was something I had never expected to do. As a dyed-in-the-wool unprogrammed Friend, I had an aversion to prepared ministry, but it was clear that God had called me to serve this meeting. Each week I asked myself, "What does it mean to be a Quaker in this meeting?" Bits and pieces of that work are sprinkled throughout this book.

Then, late in 2016, I had the opportunity to lead a weekend course at Ben Lomond Quaker Center. I had proposed the title "Primitive Quakerism Revived," and preparing for that weekend forced me to cobble together a first draft of this book. The prospect of facing the participants obliged me to try to state things clearly and concisely. Their questions and comments forced me to recast or discard many half-baked concepts and focus on what is essential to reviving Quakerism in the twenty-first century.

Charles Martin has been my editor and publisher for the last decade. His Inner Light Books has been a blessing to the Religious Society of Friends. I treasure his friendship and deeply value his advice in preparing five books together. His copy editor, Kathy McKay, has been invaluable.

Through Charles, I met David Johnson, an Australian Friend and fellow Inner Light writer. David's comments on a draft in the summer of 2017 were much appreciated. Rachel Ernst Stahlhut and Noah Merrill reviewed the penultimate draft, and each took the time to make very helpful comments.

Finally, I have to acknowledge Peggy's essential (nonmedical) support over the past several years as I worked on this book. She has commented on isolated pages and full drafts without sparing my feelings. Equally important, she has put up with my general distractedness without complaint as I have wandered about trying to get a chapter, section, paragraph, or single word just right. I don't know what I would do without her.

Introduction

William Penn wrote a Quaker classic, *Primitive Christianity Revived*, in the mid-1690s. He wrote as a Christian addressing other Christians. His premise was simple: Quakers had rediscovered Christianity as it had been originally established by Jesus and his apostles. The book was a short, carefully reasoned, and scripturally based presentation of that claim. He was calling on other Christians to give up their allegiance to various other sects and to join in a general revival of Christianity, of which the Society of Friends was the vanguard.

Penn was writing at the end of almost two centuries of religious upheaval and sectarian violence that had been touched off by Martin Luther when he sent his *Ninety-Five Theses* to the Archbishop of Mainz on October 30, 1517. Luther believed that the Catholic Church (in which he was a monk) had become overwhelmed by abusive and idolatrous practices that needed to be ended in order to reestablish Christianity on its true base. Penn endorsed Luther's proposition but declared that the Protestant Reformation had fallen short. He asserted that George Fox, an itinerant preacher and one of the founders of the Religious Society of Friends, had been raised up by God to complete the job and that the now-realized result was being practiced by Quakers. He wrote *Primitive Christianity Revived* as an invitation to all people to join him.

In recent decades, I have become concerned that Quakers in all our branches have similarly allowed their faith and practice to become encrusted with borrowed and invented traditions that need to be scraped away so that we can revive the Quakerism Fox and Penn proclaimed. This book is a call for you to join me in doing so.

Background

Like William Penn, I am a convert to the Quaker way, and like many new converts, I threw myself into service to the Society of Friends. I have been active in several monthly meetings and quarterly meetings. I have clerked my yearly meeting and tended it as field secretary. In my late forties, I quit my job and enrolled in the Quaker Studies program at the Earlham School of Religion. While there, I felt a call to minister to Friends as a writer.

Over the last two decades, my writing was concentrated first on the Quakers and Quakerism of the seventeenth century while I worked on modern English translations of some of William Penn's theological works and then on the works of Friends writing in the nineteenth century. Though there were changes in beliefs and outward activities over those two centuries, the similarities far outweighed the differences. That is not the case for the two most recent centuries. In these, the divergences from the principles and practices of our spiritual predecessors have been wide-ranging and dramatic. While a nineteenth-century Quaker might unobtrusively fit in a seventeenth-century meeting, that same individual would stand out in a contemporary Friends church or meeting.

What accounts for such notable changes? Some of the differences may be the products of divine revelation and some because different people in different times need different forms of spiritual nurture. God is gracious and meets us each where we are, providing the support that we each need, but it seemed to me that not all of the changes fall into these categories. Many of them

Introduction

occurred in relatively short periods of time when the Society was most contentious. Our lack of unity with each other must be seen as a sign that Quakers have not always been in unity with their Guide. It seems likely that many changes arose from human tendencies. They were simply things we chose to do.

In the course of contemplating these changes, I received an invitation to present a workshop at the Ben Lomond Quaker Center in California and felt drawn to propose "Primitive Quakerism Revived" as the weekend's topic. At the time, I had little more than a sense that this was something important that I needed to spend more time on. I suggested holding the weekend in early 2015. Fortunately, the Ben Lomond schedule couldn't accommodate that date and I had until November 2016 to get ready.

The course of my preparations led me to revisit Quaker writings from earlier centuries and drew me into many deep conversations with twenty-first-century Friends. In trying to shape my thoughts, I created half a dozen outlines of the weekend, but none was completely satisfying. When it came time to finalize the materials for the weekend, I realized that what was missing was a clear statement of the reasons I thought Quakers needed a revival, and I felt I should be able to state these in a one-page handout. Ten interrelated signs stood out to me. The following section is an expanded version of that document. These are the essential reasons that I have undertaken this book. Together, they are what lead me to advocate a revival in the Religious Society of Friends. These symptoms will be examined in more detail in the chapters ahead.

Ten Signs We Need a Revival

Do you have the wisdom and the heart to repent of all the things that might obstruct your service? Do you have the heart to forgive even the unforgivable? Do you have what it takes to love the unloveable, to walk and talk with those you think are your enemies? Will you be able to see everyone as belonging to the community of God and not otherwise?

Gladys Kang'ahi[1]

1. God Is Not the Center of Our Lives and Our Meetings

This is, of course, a generalization. There are many Friends who order their lives around what they feel divinely called to do, but much of our energy (including my own) is devoted to temporal affairs. We have families. We are active politically. We worry that we don't have enough money, even though we devote long hours to our jobs. There never seems to be enough time for all our busyness. We live in stress and with fears that too often threaten to overwhelm us. All of these (and more) displace us from the Quaker path, an alternative based on a direct and trusting relationship with the All-Loving Spirit.

2. Being Quaker Is Not Our Primary Identification

If you didn't tell anyone, would you be recognized as a Quaker? At one time, our outward appearance and manner of speech were distinctive. Even more than that, Friends were identifiable by their lives of faithfulness. This sometimes demanded singling ourselves out and being singled out by others. Thousands of early Friends were arrested, fined, and imprisoned. Hundreds died for the crime of being Quaker. But today we are rarely required to act in ways that make us uncomfortable, let alone make our religious affiliation too obvious.

3. The Spread of Individualism among Friends

Individualism is a dominant ideology in today's Western culture. "Personal freedom" is its idol. Capitalism and materialism bolster individualism in Western culture by esteeming financial prosperity at the cost of spiritual prosperity. This has infected, undercut, and devalued spiritual communities, including the Religious Society of Friends. If, for example, members feel they have a leading, they usually seem to believe the role of their home meeting is to support them in their chosen ministry, not to discern whether they are right in choosing it. Individualism feeds hubris—it puts each of us at the center of our lives.

4. The Redefinition of Community

The Children of the Light (an early name for Quakers) believed their community had been divinely gathered together. Their shared purpose was to model an alternative society and culture and, in doing so, to challenge others to act the same. They were building the beloved community—the kingdom of heaven on earth—and their communities stood as a testimony to the whole world.

Too often today, we see our communities solely as groups of people who voluntarily decide to gather together in order to meet our individual needs and to support each other. If that is true, the community exists to serve those inside it, not to serve God or to confront the world and dare others to join us.

5. Being Unwilling to Say What We Believe

Many Friends imagine that being a Quaker means we can believe anything—that there are no essential beliefs. Related to this is the idea that we can redefine what membership means and therefore what characterizes a church or meeting as Quaker. As a consequence, we are reluctant to state clearly and simply what it means to be a Friend. In doing so, we fail to meet the needs of our children, newcomers, and long-time members and attenders.

Many parents state that they want their children to make up their own minds about a religious affiliation but then fail to tell their children what it would mean to choose this particular option. Children want to know. In order to make an informed decision, they need and want to know what they may be accepting or rejecting. One of the greatest gifts that parents can give their children is to simply, clearly, and truthfully tell them what they believe and then trust them to make their own decisions.

Similarly, when newcomers visit our churches and meetings, they deserve clear-cut answers to their questions. To say you can believe anything or nothing fails to do that. The Friends of Truth (another early name) originally arose at a time when large numbers of people were in search of spiritual and religious homes. Those first Friends fearlessly said what they believed and, as a result, some visitors went away disappointed because it wasn't what they were seeking. We need the same courage. Not everyone is looking for what we have; helping them to find another religious affiliation may be the most loving thing we can do for them.

Likewise, even long-time attenders deserve spiritual care and guidance. A community that is unwilling to set limits and to clearly articulate its boundaries neglects the needs of its members and can impede their spiritual growth.

6. Ritualizing Meeting for Worship

Early Friends did not invent silent waiting worship. There were already congregations in the north of England that assembled in

Introduction

silence and waited for divine inspiration when George Fox first visited them. Their gatherings were acts of faith and trust in the immediate guidance of the Holy Spirit, but this no longer seems to be enough. The outside world constantly clamors for our attention, and stepping through a meetinghouse or church door does not magically transport us to a sacred place either outwardly or inwardly.

It may now be necessary to provide a time of transition from the secular to the holy, but if we allow these trappings to crowd out the time we have to encounter the Luminous directly—to still and open ourselves to the Inward Guide—we cheat ourselves out of the precious inheritance our spiritual ancestors bequeathed us.

In particular, I need to address my own tradition within the Religious Society of Friends. We hold what we call unprogrammed worship and then carve away at the time by opening the period with singing, verbal readings or the recitation of a query, or passing out printed materials. We give people something to think about, and this encourages them to stay in their heads. It holds them back from what our forebears called "centering down."

As individuals, we separate ourselves from our fellow worshippers by reading books, journaling, or following preplanned paths for meditation. Quaker worship is a community practice. Whatever we do that separates us from joining in that communion harms us and diminishes the whole body of worshippers.

Meetings are often closed with still another set of rituals. These may include the recitation of "joys and concerns" or an invitation to say things that didn't rise to the level of ministry or to offer afterthoughts.

7. Encrusting Outward Characteristics

One of the foundational principles of Quakerism was that outward practices are not essential to true religion. Early Friends held that anyone who faithfully followed the guidance of the Inward Light of Christ could be saved. They didn't have to know about Jesus or the Bible, subscribe to a particular creed, or engage in specific outward rites and rituals. This was a scandal to other Christians.

Yet today, some Friends identify Quakerism with an outward form of worship or with behaviors that were meaningful in the past but are no longer. This shows up, for example, in the use of antiquated terms as a private language with other Quakers—for example, saying "First Day" when speaking with Friends but not with non-Friends. More worrying is the formal listing of certain outward behaviors as "the testimonies" and making these the things that define what it means to be a Friend.

8. Treating Outreach as an Activity

Why do we seek new members? Is it for their sake or for our own?

In the 1650s, the early Quakers evangelized, preaching the gospel given to them by the Inward Teacher. These Publishers of Truth (a third early name by which Quakers were known) felt compelled by a burning love to spread what they had found as widely as possible. Their goal was to share this treasure with others. Although the Society gained new members at an astonishing rate, this wasn't the measure of their success. It was a side effect of their compulsion to let others know what they had been gifted.

Today, Friends often seek out new members, but we seem to be motivated by fear rather than love—fear that we will disappear, fear that our numbers won't be able to pay the rent or mortgage, or fear that we won't have enough people to do the good works we want to achieve. This is backwards. New members will come because they are drawn to us by our example. If we focus on doing the work we have been called to do, our Sustainer will send the people and the resources we will need to fulfill our mission.

9. Accommodating to the Surrounding Culture

> *I fear there is a considerable number under our name of this description, who not only love the world, but also its friendships, manners, maxims, policies, customs, fashions, vanities, pleasures, and amusements, yet like to bear the name of Quaker because it has become honorable among men. Alas! How much better would it be for the Society and the promotion of Truth if it was still a name of reproach among men!*
>
> Elias Hicks[2]

Almost two hundred years ago, Elias Hicks wrote that he feared there were Quakers who loved the "manners, maxims, policies, customs, fashions, vanities, pleasures, and amusements" of the outside world. He wrote in a time when Friends still strived to separate themselves from their neighbors. They tried to maintain a protective "hedge" around the Society of Friends, but Hicks feared some loved the ways of the world more. He was joined in this concern by Friends who otherwise disagreed with him on many issues. I can only imagine how those early-nineteenth-century Quakers would react to Christmas trees and Easter egg hunts at Friends churches and meetings.

10. Being Admired

Hicks went on to lament that "Quaker" was no longer "a name of reproach." Quakers have an impressive reputation. Our good works earned us a Nobel Peace Prize, and our rejection of slavery long before any other religious body is often fondly remembered. But admiration is an addictive and stupefying drug. It encourages us to rest on our laurels. To achieve such acclaim is a sign that the wider society considers us harmless and unthreatening. It is a sign that we are not fulfilling our calling.

Disclosures

Like all books, this one rests on sets of biases and assumptions that I make implicitly. These are usually buried so deep in my unconscious that I am largely unaware of them. As a result, they come out in my writing without my thinking about them. If a reader doesn't share them, they can become stumbling blocks to communication. They get in the way and make it difficult for the reader to hear what I am saying.

I want this book to be valuable to you whether or not you share the same assumptions. To help bridge the gap, I have tried to dig them out as much as I can. My hope is that if I list them for you, we will have a better starting point for dialogue. It has taken me quite a while to uncover and articulate the eight assumptions I have listed below. There are certainly more that I have yet to acknowledge.

1. There Is a God

> *Oh! love truth and its Testimony, whether its Witness be to you, or against you, love it, that into my Mothers house you all may come, and into the Chamber of her that conceived me, where you may embrace, and be embraced of my dearly*

Introduction

beloved one, Love is his Name, Love is his Nature, Love is his life, surelie he is the dearest and the fairest.

Sarah Blackborow[3]

First and most important, I assume that there is an Infinite Spirit who cares for us and about us. This isn't a bearded old man sitting on a cloud. My sense of God is of a spiritual being who is both intimately present in my life and far greater than I can imagine. One essential implication of this assumption is that there is divine involvement in the world and in each of our lives. This means that the Infinite Being has hopes and dreams for me, a finite creature, and for how I live my life. Living faithfully requires that, to the greatest extent I can, I discern what those divine desires are and try to fulfill them.

I understand that the use of the word 'God' can be difficult for some. They may feel the term is tainted by patriarchy or other past associations. I understand these tender spots and I will try not to poke them, but I also need to be clear. Since God is the term in widest use in the English language, it is the one most likely to be recognized by readers from a variety of backgrounds.

God is also the word for the Divine most used by our spiritual ancestors, as is reflected in the excerpts from their writings included in this book. For myself, I am comfortable using synonyms—in prayer, my preferred term is 'Beloved'—and I believe that we are enriched by the multitude of terms that have been and are used to refer to the One.

2. I Am a Christian

This has become a fault line within the Society of Friends—one that has erupted in needlessly destructive earthquakes. It would be far easier for me to avoid the subject because I know that some potential readers will stop reading at these words. William Penn wrote as a Christian to Christians, but because he was a Quaker Christian, he knew that some of his beliefs were very different from those of most of his intended readers. Even so, he hoped readers would suspend their judgments of him long enough to consider what he had to say. I am asking the same of you.

My path to admitting my Christianity is unique. I was brought up Roman Catholic and remained an active Catholic until my late twenties. When I was twenty-seven, I divorced—an act I felt was inconsistent with continued membership in that church. Soon after, I found a spiritual home within a Friends meeting that declared Christian beliefs optional. I left Catholic dogmas behind and, for a time, neither believed nor disbelieved anything about Jesus.

Being at the Earlham School of Religion challenged me to articulate what I put my faith in. I found I had great love and respect for Jesus but (like Penn) could not accept Trinitarian doctrine, although I did accept that "there are three . . . and these three are one" (1 John 5:7[*]). In the end, my convictions relied most of all on my trust in the depth of God's grace. I believe that God comes to us in different ways depending on our needs. Sometimes we need the support of a heavenly parent, and other times we need a spiritual counselor, a Paraclete, to guide us. In divine love, the Almighty comes to us in these ways. But there are other times when we need to know that God truly grasps what it is like to inhabit a human body—to wake up rough on a cold morning with aching limbs and a full bladder or to experience the sheer joy of being embodied or to suffer the terrors of facing our mortality. Through Jesus' life of faithfulness and humility, God intimately

---

[*] All Bible texts are from the King James Version.

experienced what it is to be human. When I am frail and pathetic, I know that same God is present with me.

3. I Am a Quaker

Perhaps this could go without saying, but this section is about saying what needs not be said. Just as William Penn wrote *Primitive Christianity Revived* as a Christian and to other Christians, I am writing as a Quaker to other Quakers. You may wonder what flavor of Quaker I am and, likewise, which form of primitive Quakerism I intend in the title.

The first answer is not simple. I found my second spiritual home with liberal unprogrammed Quakers, and for a while I could not imagine how those in the other branches could claim the name. I was wrong. We squabble like children fighting over our parent's will—each saying I am the true heir and each one being right. We are all true spiritual heirs of George Fox and Margaret Fell. None of us can claim to be the sole beneficiary—the true guardian of the flame and conserver of the only Truth.

I find profound spiritual succor in unprogrammed meetings for worship, but not in that way only. I have been nourished by pastored worship services as well. We have much to offer each other.

Please suspend your judgment of me and of the various outward forms of Quakerism long enough to consider what I have to say.

4. God Communicates Directly with Each Person

> *Now, with Friends ... it is a leading principle in religion, that the work of the Holy Spirit in the soul is not only immediate and direct, but perceptible. We believe that we are all furnished with an inward Guide or Monitor, who makes his voice known to us, and who, if faithfully obeyed and closely followed, will infallibly conduct us into true virtue and happiness.*
>
> Joseph John Gurney[4]

I assume the truth of this core message, which was originally articulated by Quakers in the middle of the seventeenth century. Simply stated, each person is provided with a channel for unmediated communication with the Divine. The early Quakers referred to this as the Inward Light of Christ. This Light shows everyone his or her true spiritual state, illuminates a path to faithful living, and empowers each to walk in that path. It allows me to know how the Creator yearns for me to live in relation to other people and to all of creation.

This is a theological statement about how people can come to know themselves and to live faithfully. It matches my own experience and, as a consequence, I am a Quaker. More broadly, I find it hopeful for myself and for all of humanity. I believe it is a message that needs to be sustained and shared.

5. Friends Have a Calling as a People

> *This is the word of the Lord God to you all, a charge to you all in the presence of the living God; be patterns, be examples in all countries, places, islands, nations, wherever you come; that your life and conduct may preach among all sorts of people,*

> *and to them. Then you will come to walk cheerfully over the world, answering that of God in every one; whereby in them ye may be a blessing, and make the witness of God in them to bless you: then to the Lord God you shall be a sweet savour, and a blessing.*
>
> George Fox[5]

My next assumption is that the "charge to you all in the presence of the living God" is still valid today. This divine injunction remains an active one. It continues to be our calling as a people to be patterns and examples—in other words, to model a way of being that challenges the existing order and offers a loving and God-centered alternative in its place.

We are not, however, God's only people. Other religious bodies have been called for other tasks.

6. The Society of Friends Exists Because We Serve God

Again, this may seem obvious, but it was the last of these unacknowledged assumptions that I have been able to uncover. I believe the continued existence of our Society is neither accidental nor necessary. It is not just a matter of chance, nor is it guaranteed. Friends have existed and will persist as a religious society so long as we are fulfilling the role to which we have been called. God will send us the resources we need to do the work we have been called to do.

7. Traditions Are Inevitable

> *Do not suffer yourselves to be deceived any longer by fair speeches, and flattering high notions, by which you have been blinded for many years, and led on to worship God in outside forms and customs, after the traditions and commandments of*

men, which, by imaginary imitations and consultations, they have set up for their own ends, and have made laws to bind the people to observe them, contrary to that light shining into the conscience.

James Nayler[6]

Next, I assume that meaningful corporate behaviors inevitably develop into traditions. Human institutions acquire memories in the form of traditions. These remind people of who they are, where they come from, and why they do what they do. Traditions help to bind communities together and give them a sense of purpose. But traditions evolve. Practices can acquire meanings far removed from what originally inspired them, and they may be maintained long after they have lost their initial purpose. A tradition can itself become an object of veneration. When this happens, it becomes necessary to discard the tradition.

To the Protestant Reformers, the rituals, holidays, doctrines, and practices perpetuated by the Church of Rome needed to be reexamined. In their eyes, some were meaningful, but too many had persisted long after they had been drained of spiritual significance or value to the congregants. In some cases, the Reformers believed the principles had been distorted to such a degree that they had become spiritually harmful. The Reformers' work was to clear away practices that were no longer functional and to scrape off accumulated layers of superfluous ornamentation from those traditions that were retained. The first Quakers felt they were completing this goal when they eliminated the outward rites and rituals, ministers, and ecclesiastical structures that remained associated with Protestant churches.

8. People Embellish

Beware of a disposition to add or diminish, in order to embellish a narrative; this may lead by degrees to a disregard of truth, and finally result in bitterness of soul.

William Allen[7]

Finally, people embellish. It is our nature to take simple things and strive to make them appear more elaborate and (at least to ourselves) more beautiful. Often, this is accomplished by adding on superfluous frills, flourishes, and practices we enjoy. Over time, a simple custom can become cluttered with various new and unneeded features. Frequently, the supposed enhancements grow in importance to the point where more time and energy is invested in them than in the original tradition.

We need look no further than the ever-evolving customs surrounding the celebration of Christmas to see this process in action. In the earliest years of Christianity, the birthday of Jesus was not marked by ceremonies or celebrations. The actual date is unknown (two of the gospels didn't even include an account of the birth), and it was only in the fourth century that it was designated as December 25—a day selected in an attempt to co-opt existing pagan midwinter festivals. Over the years, various ways of observing this day have come and gone.

An alien observer might believe the purpose of the holiday is not to remember a birth but to spend money, venerate evergreen trees, and remember Santa Claus. Christmas trees were adopted from ancient Germanic (pagan) winter solstice feasts—probably in about the sixteenth century—and were introduced into the United States less than two hundred years ago. Santa Claus, as we recognize him today, is a nineteenth-century conflation of a Dutch figure called *Sinterklaas* with the English Father Christmas.

History has shown that the Religious Society of Friends is no exception in the acquisition, elaboration, and embellishment of traditions. In response, Quakers have engaged in several reformations, notably one in the middle of the eighteenth century and another in the middle of the nineteenth century. It is my belief that it is time for another period of self-evaluation and reformation. This is an undertaking that starts within the Religious Society of Friends but has the potential to contribute to a spiritual awakening in the wider world. We Friends have something unique and precious to offer. In this book, I hope to recruit others to join me in taking on this task.

Chapter 1
Quaker Revival

Whether Quakerism be, as some Friends believe, destined to any considerable revival or not, it seems at least certain that any important revival of religion must be the result of a fresh recognition and acceptance of the very principles upon which the Society of Friends is built. What these principles and the practices resulting from them really are, is a subject on which there is a surprising amount of ignorance amongst us.

Caroline Stephen[1]

Religious revivals succeed when people feel the status quo no longer works and are seeking a way to more closely bond with the Infinite and with each other. Revival frequently becomes necessary when religion has been subverted by and become so entwined with the wider culture that it no longer serves to spiritually challenge or nurture its adherents. In that case, the focus of revival is on facing up to the ways that the religious body has accommodated itself to the society's customs. How has it made itself comfortable with the world's ways?

Revivals are frequently sparked in times of uncertainty and rapid external change. Israel in Christianity's first century was under Roman domination and was subject to social, economic, military, and political pressures to conform to imperial standards. Many in the Jewish establishment collaborated. This produced repeated revolts and provided a fertile environment for the incubation of a religious revival.

Similarly, the decade of English Civil Wars that started in 1642 provided an ideal setting for religious revival—war increases anxiety, and these wars were explicitly religious in nature. As in the first century, the civil wars laid bare divergences in faith and practice, highlighting the possibility of profound religious transformation.

Continental Europe had been torn by religious turmoil for over a century. Even before the beginning of the Protestant Reformation, a number of religious movements had denounced the state of Christianity and claimed to be reviving the faith that had existed in the days of the apostles. Restoring "primitive Christianity" was a primary justification for establishing a new sect. Reformers proclaimed a new beginning was needed since everyone else had it wrong. Their new religious body was going to fix everything.

There is no one definitive path to follow in a revival. "Primitive Christianity revived" looks very different depending on which aspects of early Christianity are emphasized. The characteristics of the first-century churches in Jerusalem, Antioch, Rome, and Alexandria (to name only a few) were very different from each other. Reading the Acts of the Apostles or the Epistles of Paul reveals that even in its earliest years the embryonic Christian movement contained marked differences. It took hundreds of years for a degree of uniformity to be imposed. No single form of faith was ever universally accepted, nor was there unanimous agreement on how to conduct worship. Schisms, heresies (as defined by the victors), and quarrels punctuate the early history of the Christian church. A degree of unity was achieved after Christianity became the official religion of the Roman Empire. This, however, led to the entanglement of church and state and laid the initial conditions for the future Protestant Reformation.

Chapter 1: Quaker Revival

We are living today in another time of rapid change as one technological revolution follows close on the heels of another. What had seemed to be settled economic and occupational certainties are constantly being disrupted, powering political commotion and war. Religious establishments have been rocked by the emergence of new movements—some violent and overtly political. In many countries, church and state are explicitly interlocked; in others, there are movements to link them. Sectarian conflicts, insurrections, and warfare dominate the news. As befits a time of rapid change and confusion, although there are many who believe we are living in an age of profound spiritual transformation and regeneration, there are also large numbers who are certain that the world is ready for the final rejection of formal religions.

On many levels, old certainties and old certitudes are under assault, and established religious bodies are challenged to speak to the new social and cultural circumstances. Those that cannot do so will fade away.

Two Types of Revival

Revivals pursue a variety of different ultimate goals. For my purposes, I will address the two forms that I believe are most characteristic of what has happened within the Society of Friends: utopian and radical.

Utopian Revival

A utopian revival is nostalgic for a vanished golden age (a time that may have existed only in stories). It wants to turn back the clock to those times and then stop it. Such a revival venerates tradition and denies the possibility that change from that alleged ideal may be necessary or divinely inspired. It strips away anything that is "new"—anything not dating back to the presumed lost utopia.

Just as primitive Christianity had several different theologically and geographically defined flavors, there are multiple candidates for its golden age. One of these is the first decades, when the apostles were still alive and the church in Jerusalem was still under the leadership of James, the brother of Jesus. Another is the middle of the first century, epitomized by one or more of the Greek churches established by Paul and described in his Epistles. Some Catholics suggest we look to the age of Constantine, whereas utopian Protestants can be counted on to agree on only one thing—it wasn't in the days of domination by the Church of Rome.

A utopian revival can succeed, but this occurs at the cost of being out of touch with the rest of the world. Anything from the outside is a corrupting force that needs to be held at bay. Once the faithful remnant has withdrawn, perfection has been achieved and there is nothing to be gained from any more interaction with "outsiders" than is absolutely necessary.

In response to the intrasocietal conflicts among Friends, several self-declared "Primitive Quaker" groups arose in the nineteenth century. They disavowed the rest of the world and all others who claimed to be Friends. Each one attempted to return to a lost golden age. Their common goal was to restore what they saw as the purity of the earliest Quakers. To do so, they rejected Hicksite, Orthodox, and Wilburite Friends,[*] viewing them as

---

[*] After two major separations in the first half of the nineteenth century, the Religious Society of Friends was comprised of three primary branches. In very rough terms, today's descendants of the Hicksites are liberal unprogrammed Friends, the Orthodox gave birth to various forms of pastoral Friends, and the Wilburites begat Conservative Friends. For a more complete description of how the branches of the Religious Society of

compromised by new ideas and innovations. And they were right. None of the major branches was the desired perfect restoration of the seventeenth-century Society of Friends. These meetings rarely survived for long, although small communities are reported to still exist.[2]

The birth mothers and fathers of Quakerism were not utopian revivalists. Although they started with an idealized vision of reestablishing primitive Christianity, they did not advocate a return to the outward practices of first-century Christians. Moreover, they rejected the notion that divine revelation had come to an end. Since they believed that direct communication with God endured to their day and would carry on into the future, change was inevitable and the golden age could be found in the present, continually evolving and unfolding.

Radical Revival

A radical revival attempts to get to the vital root ('radical' derives from *radix*, the Latin word for 'root'). This form of revival seeks to identify the underlying principles that define and shape the body and restore them. Like the roots of a plant, these principles may be hidden from view, and some adherents may not be aware of them or of their significance.

Like pruning a tree, a radical revival seeks to remove the obscuring debris and cut off foreign grafts to reveal the healthy root stock. In doing so, it may need to trim away some of the visible foliage (outward beliefs and practices) in order to restore what is fundamental to its proper place. To the extent that people

---

Friends have evolved, see Thomas Hamm, *The Quakers in America* (New York: Columbia University Press, 2003).

identify their sense of religion with the lopped-off religious rituals and practices, they will resist the revival.

The seventeenth-century Publishers of Truth were radical revivalists. They believed the Protestant Reformation had fallen short of returning Christianity to its roots. They stripped away virtually all of the outward practices in worship and in ecclesiastical structure. It must have been especially difficult to discontinue long-held, comfortable, and comforting practices, but, in doing so, they believed they were recovering what was inwardly essential.

The Nature of Revival among Friends

Now, if you will know the Way to Sion, *turn your Faces thitherward, and turn your Minds to* That *of God, which joyns to the Lord; which calls your Minds in, out of the visible and outward things, unto that which is inward and invisible: For God is an invisible God, and no Mortal Eye can behold him; and that Eye, which sees God, is invisible; and that Ear that hears God, is invisible, and that which worships God, is invisible; and the House where the Lord God is worshipped, is invisible: And this you shall witness to be the way to* Sion, *if ever you know it, or find it.*

Margaret Fell[3]

It took courage to be part of the revival Jesus initiated in the first century, and it took courage to be a Quaker in the seventeenth century. In both instances, the revivalists attracted persecution for their beliefs. In both, people were challenged to give up outward practices that had been their religious inheritance for centuries. Both called on people to sacrifice prized customs and traditions. When people joined the new spiritual movement, they surrendered much that was comfortable, familiar, and pleasant in favor of what

Chapter 1: Quaker Revival

must have felt like an austere new expression of the divine message. Being like other people would have been far easier. It will take courage to follow their examples in the twenty-first century.

The book in your hands is not a call to pitch revival tents in our churchyards or on our meetinghouse lawns. That might be good and, if it happens, so be it, but that is an outward exercise. Revival in the Religious Society of Friends must necessarily be focused on the inward.

Likewise, this is not a call for contemporary Quakers to put on the trappings of the seventeenth century. When primitive Friends claimed they were reviving primitive Christianity, they rejected the elegant clothing, flattering speech, and popular forms of worship of their day but did not replace these with the dress, language, or worship style of first-century Christians. Their task was to discern the essential principles that animated the Christian movement in its earliest days and then to live in accordance with those values in the social, economic, and cultural circumstances in which they lived. The consequences of those inward principles molded the outward forms that came to characterize them.

George Fox challenged the Children of the Light to be patterns and examples for those living around them. In response, some did "walk cheerfully over the world," preaching the gospel that had been placed in their mouths, but their most effective recruitment instrument was the example of their conduct: their behavior and character. Their ordinary, everyday lives witnessed to their faith.

This book calls on Quakers today to do the same: to repossess the essential principles that energized and strengthened those Friends of Truth, to apply those principles to the various societies and cultures we live in around the world and, once again to be patterns and examples to our neighbors. Our speech, clothes, and forms of worship will be different from those of our spiritual ancestors—and different from each other—but we aren't called to preach merely by means of outward forms. Only lives quickened by faithfulness will speak compellingly.

Chapter 2
In the Beginning

The Quaker movement arose in the midst of two decades of enormous political upheaval and religious violence in the British Isles—a period of sectarian strife that in some ways resembled the chaos in Iraq and Syria at the time I am writing. In broad strokes, the 1640s were the years of the English Civil Wars, which reached a climax with the execution of Charles I in 1649. The 1650s saw the establishment of a short-lived parliamentary Commonwealth, soon supplanted by a thinly disguised military dictatorship and a period of steadily increasing internal instability. The decade ended with the restoration of the monarchy under Charles II in 1660.

In this era, relationships between church and state were very different from those today. Many if not most people in England (as in the rest of Christendom) assumed that one church would be "established" as the official national church and that every loyal subject would be a member of that church. The English king or queen was the head of the government and of the Church of England. After the execution of Charles I, Parliament took exclusive control of government, instituted Puritan[*] principles within the official church, abolished the bishops, and reorganized the structure of the church. Once the monarchy had been restored,

---

[*] Puritans were Calvinist (Reformed) Protestants who believed that the Church of England had retained too much of its Catholic heritage.

Charles II reestablished the Church of England as it had been under his father.

Quakers (in agreement with other religious dissenters at the time) rejected the beliefs, practices, and structures of both Anglicans and Puritans. This led to a period of official persecution during which thousands of Friends were jailed and hundreds died. It was only after 1689 that Quakers were legally allowed to build their own meetinghouses and worship together. The experience of surviving nearly half a century of civil war and persecution marked the faith and practice of the incipient Society of Friends.*

The work of many early Friends was essential to that Society's survival. Three are highlighted below. George Fox, from the first generation, is often credited as the Society's founder. Two others from the second generation, Robert Barclay and William Penn, produced theological statements that both articulated and shaped the Society's system of beliefs and practices.

George Fox

He [George Fox] was a Man that God endued with a Clear and Wonderful *Depth: A Discerner of other's Spirits, and very much a* Master *of his own . . . And* indeed, *it shewed, beyond all Contradiction, that* God sent him; *in that* no Art or Parts had any Share in the Matter or Manner of his Ministry; *and that so many* Great Excellent, *and* Necessary Truths, *as he came forth to Preach to Mankind, had therefore nothing of Man's Wit or Wisdom to recommend*

---

* I refer to the early Quaker movement as the "Society of Friends" (or "the Society") even though that term does not appear in print until early in the eighteenth century. The term "Religious Society of Friends" did not appear until late in the eighteenth century.

Chapter 2: In the Beginning

them. So that as to Man he was an Original, *being* no Man's Copy.

William Penn[1]

No examination of the beginnings of Quakerism can ignore George Fox (1624–1691). He provided the Religious Society of Friends with its initial footing. Fox was born in 1624 to solidly Puritan parents in the village of Fenny Drayton in central England. George was a spiritually precocious youth who was increasingly uncomfortable with the religious state of his country, and he became estranged from the various denominations of his day. He sought to know God and to know God's will for him. Fox left home in 1643 to seek spiritual guidance and wandered about the war-ravaged countryside seeking out those who were educated and considered to be gifted religious leaders. In 1647, he had an "opening" (a spontaneous moment of spiritual insight) into why none could help him. As he later wrote in his *Journal*:

> Now after I had received that opening from the Lord that to be bred at Oxford or Cambridge was not sufficient to fit a man to be a minister of Christ, I regarded the priests less, and looked more after the dissenting people. . . . But as I had forsaken all the priests, so I left the separate preachers also, and those called the most experienced people; for I saw there was none among them all that could speak to my condition. And when all my hopes in them and in all men were gone, so that I had nothing outwardly to help me, nor could tell what to do, then, Oh then, I heard a voice which said, 'There is one, even Christ Jesus, that can speak to thy condition' and when I heard it my heart did leap for joy.[2]

In other words, only God can prepare and qualify anyone to be a minister. Education alone is insufficient preparation to serve God, and formal ministers aren't needed for people to know God. Not only *could* Christ speak to his condition, Fox also declared that

29

Christ had "come to teach his people himself."[3] That is to say, everyone has immediate access to divine guidance. No intermediary—church, priest, elder, minister, or anyone else, regardless of training—is necessary.

The implications of this revelation struck directly at the temporal power and authority of the established church. While the Anglicans had rejected the Pope and the Puritans sought to dispense with priests and bishops, Fox saw no need even for the pastor of a local congregation nor for the payment of tithes to support the official church. If all have equal access to the Infinite Spirit, then all are equally empowered to read the scriptures and to preach. During simple, unstructured meetings held to worship God, the farmer, seamstress, laborer, servant girl, and local lord can all sit together on the same spiritual footing. And if ordained celebrants aren't needed, neither are their accessories. Elaborate vestments convey no spiritual authority. Incense burning in a censor and wine in a gold chalice are mere material things, not consecrated substances in holy vessels. These are human frills extraneous to true Christianity. Like Jesus cleansing the temple, early Friends saw themselves as stripping away all the worldly rites and rituals that had been grafted onto and obscured the original Christianity established by Jesus and the apostles.

This insight was a turning point in George Fox's life. Through a series of further openings, he was led to a new articulation of the Christian message. These revelations transformed this wandering religious searcher into an intentional traveling minister. Over the next forty years, he preached throughout England and undertook missionary journeys to Scotland, Wales, Ireland, Barbados, Jamaica, British colonies in North America, the Netherlands, and Germany. Although he was far from alone in providing leadership

Chapter 2: In the Beginning

to the first generations of Friends, George Fox is deservedly credited as the founder of the Quaker movement.

Early on, Fox acted as if he were living in the end times foretold in the Book of Revelation. Some Protestants at that time believed they were living through the scriptural signs and wonders that heralded an outward second coming of Christ and the end of the world as it was known. Fox sometimes sounded as if he agreed with them. Under those circumstances, the greatest imperative would be to spread the word as widely and quickly as possible in order to spiritually awaken as many people as possible before it was too late.

To some, Friends seemed poised to convert the whole world in their lifetimes. In the 1650s, the budding Society grew rapidly—so quickly that it sparked concern among the political and ecclesiastic authorities. Quakers were identified as dangerous radicals who might even threaten the establishment. When royal government was restored in 1660, it imposed stringent restrictions on religious dissenters, singling out Friends for further oppression starting with the Quaker Act of 1662.

George Fox spent much of the 1660s in prison, and by the time he was released in 1666, he had revised his strategy for the young Society. Although Quaker missionary efforts did not stop, spreading the message God had entrusted to Friends was paired with work to build the institutional structures needed to endure years of persecution. It was clear that Jesus wasn't soon coming again in the flesh and that Quaker missionaries were not going to convert the whole world. The Society needed to prepare to coexist with others in a fallen world.

Fox urged Friends to create formal connections between local worship groups. Several of these were linked together to conduct business once a month. These were dubbed 'monthly meetings.' The monthly meetings in a wider geographic area sent representatives every three months to 'quarterly meetings,' and each quarter named representatives to an annual 'yearly meeting.' One yearly meeting gathered each year in London for the Isle of Britain, another met in Dublin for Ireland, and several more were established in the American colonies. This structure was very similar to the sessions, presbyteries, synods, and general assemblies of the Presbyterian Church. Each yearly meeting was independent, although Philadelphia Yearly Meeting held informal authority over the other American meetings and London Yearly Meeting was recognized as first among equals.

One innovation caused controversy and an early split in the Quaker movement. Fox established separate business meetings at the monthly meeting level for women. Friends were clear that in Christ there is no male or female and that a woman preaching or evangelizing was not a problem—the Inward Teacher could select and prepare anyone to minister—but for some Quakers, granting women a share in leadership or authority (even in a business meeting separate from that of the men) was unacceptable. It took more than a decade for the issue to be settled and the rift healed, and this required the disownment or death of several prominent opponents. Over the next century, woman's quarterly and yearly business meetings were established.

In the course of his life, George Fox wrote numerous letters, epistles, pamphlets, and tracts in support of the nascent movement. Most important for future generations is *The Journal of George Fox*, an account of Fox's openings and travels that was assembled by Thomas Ellwood after Fox's death. This was not a daily journal but a compilation of two partial accounts Fox had

Chapter 2: In the Beginning

dictated in the 1670s and 1680s that Ellwood supplemented with other materials.

George Fox was not a systematic theologian. In preaching and in writing, his intent was primarily evangelical and pastoral—calling, encouraging, admonishing, and guiding. Although a general understanding of his religious beliefs can be extracted from his works, two younger men, Robert Barclay (1648–1690) and William Penn (1644–1718) wrote the descriptions of seventeenth-century Quaker doctrines and theology that came to be viewed as definitive.

It is important to remember that theological diversity characterized the first decades of the Religious Society of Friends. Although George Fox encouraged the work of both Robert Barclay and William Penn, the theologies they described differ from what Fox wrote or what other early Quakers (most of whom did not have theological training) had written. Nor do Barclay and Penn agree with each other in all cases.

Robert Barclay

Not by strength of arguments, or by a particular disquisition of each doctrine, and convincement of my understanding thereby, came [I] to receive and bear witness of the truth, but by being secretly reached by this life; *for when I came into the* silent assemblies *of God's people, I felt a* secret power *among them, which touched my heart, and as I gave way unto it, I found the evil weakening in me, and the good raised up, and so I became thus knit and united unto them.*

Robert Barclay[4]

Robert Barclay, the second laird[*] of Ury, came from the Scottish gentry. His theological preparation was extensive. Born into a Presbyterian family, he was taught strict Calvinist doctrines as a boy. In his adolescence, he received theological training at the Scots College in Paris, a Jesuit refuge for exiled Scottish Catholics, where his uncle (also named Robert Barclay) was the rector. On returning to Scotland, however, he discovered Quakers and, in 1666, declared himself a Friend.

Barclay became one of the most articulate advocates of the Society of Friends, writing several major scholarly defenses of Quakerism in his short life. Of greatest consequence is *An Apology for the True Christian Divinity* (often referred to simply as "Barclay's Apology"). This was first published in Latin in 1676 and in English two years later. The book is organized into fifteen propositions (theological topics) and lays out a systematic rebuttal of the Calvinist theology then dominant in Scotland and among English Puritans. For the next two centuries, the *Apology* remained the standard reference for Quaker theology, and it is still available today.[5]

In addition to his writing, Barclay served Friends as part of a consortium that bought the East Jersey colony in hopes of creating a safe haven for Quakers in North America. He was appointed governor of East Jersey, although he never crossed the Atlantic to visit the settlement. Robert Barclay died in 1690 when he was forty-two years old.

---

[*] In Scotland, a laird is the hereditary owner of a large estate who has been officially recognized by the Lord Lyon King of Arms. The laird is not a noble title, but it does rank above a gentleman or esquire.

Chapter 2: In the Beginning

William Penn

Our Worthy Friend, William Penn, was known to be a Man of great Abilities, of an Excellent Sweetness of Disposition, quick of Thought, and of a ready Utterance, full of the Qualification of True Discipleship, Even Love without Dissimulation; as extensive in Charity, as comprehensive in Knowledge: Malice or Ingratitude were utter Strangers to him, being so ready to forgive Enemies, that the Ungrateful were not excepted; so that he may justly be rank'd among the Learned, Good and Great. . . . In fine, he was Learn'd without Vanity, Apt without Forwardness, Facetious in Conversation, yet weighty and Serious; of an Extraordinary Greatness of Mind, yet void of the Stain of Ambition.

Anonymous[6]

William Penn is best remembered today as the founder of Pennsylvania. He was the son of Admiral William Penn, an upper-class Englishman who was an admiral and general at sea in the English Commonwealth navy and, nimbly switching sides, also served in the restored royal government as a member of Parliament and a commissioner of the Navy Board (in modern terms, roughly equivalent to the United States Secretary of the Navy). In the course of his career, the admiral became close friends with two kings, Charles II and James II. His son was later to benefit from these relationships.

The younger Penn was exceptionally well educated. As a young man, he received theological training in France at Saumur, the principal Huguenot academy in the seventeenth century. Returning to England, he studied law in London.

Like Barclay, William Penn was a talented writer, but his interests were broader. In addition to defenses of "the People call'd *Quakers*," he wrote influential political works, travelogues, and collections of advice and aphorisms. Whereas Barclay wrote for a theologically sophisticated audience (sometimes in Latin), Penn's works were aimed at a mass audience. His goal was not merely to articulate and defend Quaker principles but to persuade non-Friends of their validity and to convince the government that Quakers posed no threat.

Like many new converts to a religious body, William Penn was a zealot and a true believer. This is evident in his writing, especially in his younger years, and his work illustrates some of the doctrinal diversity that characterized the Society of Friends at that time. His first Quaker text, *Truth Exalted: To Princes, Priests and People*, announced that Quakers were the only true Christians (a view shared by many other early Friends) and that all others were only "so-called Christians." Next he penned a polemic, *The Sandy Foundation Shaken*, for which he was accused of blasphemy and thrown into the Tower of London.

Penn's intention in *The Sandy Foundation Shaken* was to expose all the superfluous human additions that had been appended to Christianity over the centuries. Quakers, he wrote, were engaged in stripping away these accumulations in order to expose the simple beauty of Christianity as it existed in its earliest, primitive form. One rejected doctrine in particular drew the attention of ecclesiastical and government authorities; it is listed in the subtitle as the doctrine "Of One God subsisting in three distinct and separate Persons." Penn attacked Trinitarian doctrine as an unbiblical human innovation. The word "trinity" does not appear in the Bible, and the doctrine was devised centuries after the death of the last person to have heard Jesus preach. Although Penn

Chapter 2: In the Beginning

believed in the triune God—Father, Son, and Holy Spirit—his opponents claimed that denial of Trinitarian doctrine amounted to a denial of the divinity of Christ. It was for this that he was imprisoned.

While in the Tower, Penn answered his opponents with another pamphlet, *Innocency with Her Open Face*. This time the subtitle was "Presented by Way of Apology for the Book Entitled The Sandy Foundation Shaken." You will, of course, notice the word "apology" in the subtitle—the same word frequently used to describe Robert Barclay's masterwork. Quakers understood Penn's pamphlet to be an apology in the theological sense, that is, as an exposition and defense of religious beliefs. In fact, the beliefs in it are no different from those in *The Sandy Foundation Shaken*, but to those who wanted to have him released (such as Admiral Penn and the admiral's good friend King Charles), "apology" could be construed as an admission of regret and the work as a retraction. The younger Penn was released after eight months of imprisonment.

The friendship of Penn's father with the king gained Penn access to the royal court, where his opinions and advice came to be highly respected. Later, he came to be one of the most valued advisers to James II. He took advantage of this royal access to lobby tirelessly for religious tolerance and an end to persecution, but his influence at court ended when King James II was overthrown in 1688. Because of his close relationship with the deposed king, Penn was forced to go into hiding, and for a time he lost control of Pennsylvania. Ironically, the "Glorious Revolution" that unseated his patron cleared the way for Parliament to pass the Act of Toleration in 1689. Although this act did not grant true religious freedom, it ended the persecution of Quakers. Under its terms, Friends could build meetinghouses without fear that they would be torn down and could worship together safe from arrest. It would still be more than a century before Quakers achieved full civil rights in Great Britain.

In lobbying for religious tolerance, Penn continued to advocate the same basic beliefs that he had earlier, but his emphasis shifted. He no longer underscored the claim that Quakers were the only true Christians or that they rejected what others considered orthodox beliefs (e.g., the Trinitarian doctrine); instead, he presented Friends as a small part of the body of Christ. What Penn achieved was toleration, not acceptance. In exchange, Quakers agreed to tolerate the beliefs of others.

Penn continued to write theological works aimed at a non-Quaker audience. In one, *Primitive Christianity Revived*, he laid out in a few dozen pages one of the best descriptions ever written of the essential principles, beliefs, and practices of seventeenth-century Friends.

Three topics are especially relevant to this book:

- the Inward Light
- worship in Spirit and in Truth
- the marks of a true Christian

The Inward Light

> *THAT which the People call'd* Quakers *lay down, as a Main Fundamental in Religion, is this,* That God, through Christ, hath placed a Principle in every Man, to inform him of his Duty, and to enable him to do it; and that those that Live up to this Principle, are the People of God, and those that Live in Disobedience to it, are not God's People, whatever Name they may bear, or Profession

Chapter 2: In the Beginning

they may make of Religion. *This is their Ancient, First, and Standing Testimony: With this they began, and this they bore, and do bear to the World.*

William Penn[7]

In *Primitive Christianity Revived*, Penn unequivocally declared that Quakerism was Christian and Protestant but differed from all other forms of Christianity in the Friends' doctrine of the Inward Light of Christ. This is the "Principle" Penn referred to in the text quoted above. This Light is not a human capability; it is not the conscience. It is not God, but it belongs to God, comes from God, and, as described in John 1:9 as "the true Light, which lighteth every man that cometh into the world." A full description of the Light Within and its actions is given in chapter 3.

Worship in Spirit and in Truth

As the Fingers shoot out of the Hand, and the Branches from the Body of the Tree; So True Religion, in all the Parts and Articles of it, Springs from this Divine Principle in Man.

William Penn[8]

One of the most obvious "Parts" that grew organically from the principle of the Inward Light was the manner in which the first Friends worshipped. According to that "Main Fundamental in Religion," each person is in direct contact with the Holy Spirit, eliminating any need for human intermediaries—no priest or minister was required to conduct the worship. Quakers asserted that when they gathered together, they were worshipping "in spirit and truth," as Jesus had directed in John 4:23–24.

The Marks of a True Christian

And dearly Beloved, live at Peace among your selves, and wait for the Spirit of Love and Concord to spring in all your Souls, that the true Mark of Christ's Disciples may appear among you.

John Burnyeat[9]

Most Christians in the seventeenth century believed that certain outward acts had the power to bring a person closer to the divine source of our being—notably the physical performance of the sacraments. For Friends, this seemed to imply that human actions could to some degree control God. For example, many Christians assumed that sprinkling or pouring water over an infant changed the child's fundamental spiritual status and required God to accept that changed relationship. Likewise, they claimed that consuming ritually prepared bread and wine created a state of communion with the Divine. But the All-Knowing is not subject to our direction—rather, it is the other way around. There are no actions that in themselves bring us close to God. On the contrary, being close to God can compel us to act in new and different ways.

Minding the Inward Light of Christ resulted in a variety of transformed outward behaviors in early Friends' day-to-day lives. Penn lists these as the marks or characteristics of true Christians.

Penn identified true Christians as:

- against tithes
- against all swearing
- against all war among Christians
- against the greetings of the times
- for plainness in speech

Chapter 2: In the Beginning

- against mixed marriages[*]
- for plainness in apparel and furnishings
- against worldly sports and pastimes
- against the observance of so-called holy days, public fasts, or feasts
- called to act blamelessly in dealing with all others and faithfully in dealing with each other
- dedicated in taking up collections to meet the needs of widows, orphans, and the helpless
- careful in taking marriages under their care
- faithful in holding regular business meetings in order to provide care and conduct business

His objective was not to produce a definitive list of Quaker commandments or of the virtues of Quakers but to describe how these people had been transformed when they opened themselves to the Inward Light flowing into their hearts. You will notice that most of the characteristics listed were not things to do but worldly acts to avoid, such as shunning flattery and refusing to pay tithes. Because of the actions of the Light working within them, primitive Friends found they could no longer engage in such outward behaviors. As we will see, this often got them in trouble.

Some Essential Concepts

As a final piece of background, it will be helpful to have an understanding of several interrelated concepts to better comprehend the Quakerism of early Friends.

---

[*] In the seventeenth century, a mixed marriage was one between a member of one religious sect and another.

The God or Spirit of the World

Though the Change from Day to Night, is by a Motion so gradual as scarcely to be perceived, yet when Night is come we behold it very different from the Day; and thus as People become wise in their own Eyes, and prudent in their own Sight, Customs rise up from the Spirit of this World, and spread by little, and little, till a Departure from the Simplicity that there is in Christ becomes as distinguishable as Light from Darkness, to such who are crucified to the World.

John Woolman[10]

Primitive Quakers did not doubt the existence of spiritual forces for good and evil that might be personified as angels, devils, or demons. Although the phrase "the spirit of the world" occurs only once in scripture (1 Corinthians 2:12), it caught the attention of the early Friends and is referenced many times in their writings. For them, this spirit was real, malign, seductive, and grievously dangerous. It offered wealth, power, and recognition to those who accepted it into their hearts and their souls. It was a vital personification of wickedness, greed, ravenousness, insatiable appetites, and self-indulgence. The god of this world was the embodiment of Spiritual Darkness. It existed in opposition to God's desire that all people live with each other in peace and harmony, mercy, joy, and justice.

Many Quakers today are distinctly uncomfortable with the idea that there is a spiritual world inhabited by supernatural beings and may find it difficult to comprehend what this meant in the seventeenth century. Even if we cannot intellectually accept the existence of angels and demons, we may come to understand what the early Quakers meant by analogy. We talk easily about the spirit of Christmas without implying that we still believe in Santa Claus.

Chapter 2: In the Beginning

The Christmas spirit is a realizing potential for goodwill, kindness, generosity, and love that celebrating Christmas can bring out in people.

Evil is at least as real as Christmas. In the week before I wrote this, a convoy of trucks carrying relief supplies to people trapped in a war zone was attacked. Dozens of drivers and aid workers were killed, and tons of desperately needed food and medicine were destroyed. This was truly wicked, and it surely arose from the workings of the spirit of this world. It is real. I know that same spirit is constantly in search of a toehold within me. If I fail to recognize, acknowledge, and resist it, I am lost.

The Lamb's War

> *Whatever the God of the world hath begotten in mens hearts to practise or to plead for, which God did not place there, all this the lamb and his followers war against. . . . Indeed their war is against the whole work and device of the God of this world, his laws, his customs, his fashions, his inventions, and all which are to add to, or take from the work of God.*
>
> James Nayler[11]

The Children of the Light emerged in the midst of vicious religious wars in England and on the continent of Europe. These had been touched off in the sixteenth century by the Protestant Reformation and already had persisted on and off for more than a century. Both Catholic and Protestant state churches embraced the use of military force to achieve the interwoven goals of church and state. The English Civil Wars were as much between different visions of Christianity as they were about the form of government. In a sense, the Lamb's War was another episode in these wars, albeit very different in form.

Until 1689, Friends in England were subject to laws forbidding them to worship in community, to build meetinghouses, or to preach the message given to them. Traveling ministers were arrested as vagrants. Thousands of Quakers were imprisoned, and hundreds died as a result of persecution. The Lamb's War constituted the Quaker opposition to this malicious use of power by governmental and church authorities. It was an ongoing nonviolent struggle, fought with spiritual weapons.

In its narrowest sense, the Lamb's War referred to Friends' resistance to legal persecution, but defiance of religious tyranny was only one facet of a broader confrontation with the evil they encountered every day. In their eyes, they were resisting a false church with a false clergy that was marked by moral degeneracy, false outward rites and rituals, and invented doctrines. This church was supported by a government that enforced the collection of tithes to pay church expenses and selectively outlawed dissenting religious bodies. The power of the state was employed to maintain the prerogatives of the established church, and in return the official church provided religious cover for the government.

In a broader sense, resistance to both official and socially enforced forms of injustice was an aspect of the Lamb's War that was fought throughout the course of everyday interpersonal relations. How you greeted people on the street or addressed a social superior and how you conducted business in the marketplace were frontline engagements in this struggle. Through the Lamb's War, the young Society of Friends presented an alternative way of living in every human endeavor.

Chapter 2: In the Beginning

In short, the Lamb's War challenged the pride, immorality, and will-worship[*] that they saw as rampant in English society.

Buying and Selling in the Seventeenth Century

They were at a Word *in Dealing: Nor could their Customers, with many Words tempt them from it, having more regard to* Truth *than* Custom, *to* Example *than* Gain.

William Penn[12]

How Quakers conducted business offers one particularly good example of how the Lamb's War was waged.

Three hundred and fifty years ago, most purchases were made at small shops owned and operated by someone in the local community. Often the proprietor family lived in rooms attached to the shop. In any business, pricing is of critical importance. Too high and customers go elsewhere; too low and you go bankrupt.

Prices were customarily settled by haggling. Merchants knew their customers and would use that knowledge in arriving at a price. They might offer to charge one amount to a member of the aristocracy and a different one to a commoner. Either way, this was just an opening bid. The merchant routinely named a price he or she knew to be too high. The purchaser was expected to counter that offer and continue to bargain until buyer and seller mutually agreed on a price. On the surface, this seems to be a fair way to deal with others—until and unless both sides agree, there is no deal. In a perfect world, that might be true, but not all buyers have the same skill at haggling, not all have the same maturity, and not all have the same civil or social authority. Some people are good

---

[*] Will-worship is putting your own will above God's will; that is, making an idol of your own desires, predilections, and ambitions.

45

liars. In general, the clever and powerful could expect to pay less and the weak and unskilled to pay more. Quaker merchants would have known such injustice from personal experience.

As a Spirit-led alternative, Friends in the marketplace adopted "the fixed price system." Each item was assigned a price that reflected, to the extent possible, its inherent value. Once that price was determined, "they were at a word"; all purchasers would be asked to pay the same amount with no room to bargain. The intention was to treat all equally and, therefore, justly. If the set price was unacceptable to a customer, the merchant was willing to lose the sale and let the shopper go elsewhere. In Penn's words, they had "more regard to Truth than Custom."

In this case, a victory was achieved in the Lamb's War. As a consequence of setting fixed prices, Quaker merchants were trusted in a way that other vendors were not. It became well known that a small child sent to buy bread from a Quaker baker or a candle from a Quaker chandler would pay the same price as anyone else. Although this was not the original intent of setting a single price, such confidence gave Friends a competitive advantage, and fixed prices spread through the marketplace.

The Kingdom of Heaven on Earth

See here a kingdom of God on the earth; it is nothing else but a kingdom of meer love, where all hurt and destroying is done away, and every work of enmity changed into one united power of heavenly love – but observe again and again, whence this comes to pass, that God's kingdom on earth is, and can be nothing else, but the power of reigning love.

Anthony Benezet[13]

Chapter 2: In the Beginning

In many Christian writings, the "kingdom of heaven" is assumed to be a spiritual paradise that good people enter after death. No doubt this was how some early Friends thought of it, too, but many believed that the Society had been called into existence so that they could build the kingdom of God on earth. One way in which some thought this would be accomplished was by the advent of the second coming of Christ. Some seventeenth-century English Christians believed they were living in the end times described in the Book of Revelation. To them, the beheading of King Charles I vacated the English throne, and they anticipated that King Jesus would soon come to claim it and establish an earthly kingdom. The restoration of the Stuart monarchy in 1660 crushed those dreams.

Although it became clear that no outward heavenly kingdom was going to be established, Quakers believed they could live in ways that made an inward kingdom of God real. By following the guidance of the Inward Light, they could contribute to the growth of the peaceable kingdom within their souls. This was a present (though hidden) reality that could be identified with the promises in chapters 4 and 5 of John's gospel of a time that was both coming and was already present. Or, as George Fox wrote in a 1658 epistle, "the church in her glory and beauty is appeared and appearing."[14] Quakers could live inwardly in the kingdom of heaven even though their outward bodies were in the kingdom of England.

This beloved inward community was outwardly embodied in a fellowship of people who were just, kind, generous, joyful, and loving. Widows and orphans were looked after. Quakers established the Sufferings Fund to help those who were imprisoned or who suffered heavy fines for their faithfulness as well as the families of those who died as a result of persecution. Besides caring for each other, they modeled how to live justly with their neighbors—treating all fairly and equally and forswearing physical violence and coercion.

Salvation

> *And all that are saved must be gathered in unto the Light of the Covenant of Life, in which is perfect Peace, and Joy, and fellowship with the Father is known by all who dwell and walk in the Light; and here stands the Unity of the Saints in Light.*
> *Dorothy White*[15]

For Christians, salvation is a core principle and the ultimate goal of our life on earth. Christians believe Jesus came into the world so that people could be saved and that this life is a probationary period—we live our mortal lives in order to qualify for life eternal.

In this respect, early Friends were no exception. Even a cursory reading of early Quaker writings will reveal that they were deeply concerned with salvation. This was not a metaphorical or allegorical concept. To be saved was ultimately to enter into heaven after death. To them, salvation encompassed several related beliefs.

First, salvation was necessary. People sin, and, by so doing, they alienate themselves from God. Sin is an act of willful deceit; it is putting our own desires first—ahead of what God wants for us and from us. This estranges the creature from the Creator. For Quakers, reconciliation is strictly an inward event. Friends did not have an outward baptism ceremony to wash away the stain of an original sin, nor was there a ritual (for example, the Anglican Sacrament of Reconciliation) by which people could confess their sins and have them forgiven.

Chapter 2: In the Beginning

Second, Jesus died for our sins, but this did not mean that people would be automatically saved by his death. By dying, Jesus made salvation possible (in traditional terms, his death "justifies" people in the eyes of God), but for an individual to be saved, she or he needs to faithfully follow the guidance of the Inward Light (by which a person becomes "sanctified"). This is constant work. As Matthew 6:34 reminds us, each day holds its own store of troubles and temptations. Backsliding is a constant threat for every human creature. Reconciliation requires repentance and conversion, a genuine change of heart that is demonstrated thereafter by the way a person lives.

Many contemporary Quakers struggle with the concept of sin. In some cases, this is the product of their experience as members of other churches where they felt shamed and humiliated by the label of sinner. This may have been paired with an image of a vengeful God and the claim that only by following the dictates of that denomination could they be protected from the eternal torture they deserved.

The first Friends did not privilege their own members or Christians in general. They asserted that the Comforter's love is universal, that the Light Within could guide everyone to a life of faithfulness and hereafter into everlasting paradise. The declaration that everyone ever born is freely offered this guidance is the most important belief differentiating Quakers from many other Christians.

This means an individual may be saved even if he or she has no knowledge of Christ or the Bible or the doctrines of Christianity. A person doesn't even have to believe in God. The Inward Light reveals our failings to all of us, points the way to salvation, and offers to empower each of us to stay on that path. But to faithfully follow that guidance requires acknowledging and renouncing our sins. This sounds like an act of will—we decide to "be good." On the contrary, it is surrendering, giving up our own hopes and dreams, and instead seeking what God desires for us. Reconciliation is an ongoing surrender of our own will.

Today, there is a multiplicity of beliefs about the afterlife. Some believe that a traditional heavenly paradise awaits where we will be greeted by those who died before us and in which we will live forever. Others expect to experience a purely spiritual union in which their sense of personhood is subsumed into the oneness of the Eternal Being. Others are unsure what, if anything, lies ahead.

Regardless of what is to come, the guidance of the Inward Light is available to lead each person in faithful living. Salvation is walking in the Light every day. If this world is all there is, that life will have contributed to the unfolding of the covenant community. It will have testified. If another life is waiting, following the Inward Guide will have prepared us for it.

Perfection

And so they go on, and preach up sin, that none can be free from sin, so long as they are upon earth, and impossibility of perfection, and so they get the Apostles and Christs words, and quite deny that which they spoke for, preached and prayed for, and laboured for, which was to present every man perfect in Christ Jesus.

Margaret Fell[16]

Closely related to salvation is the question of whether people in this world are capable of perfection. Early Friends utterly rejected the concept of human depravity. Sin is not our natural state. It is not inevitable, and ministers who claimed it was were, in Margaret Fell's words, "preaching up sin."

The early Quakers believed that when Jesus said "Be ye therefore perfect" (Matthew 5:48), it was as much a commandment as "Thou shalt not kill." This is a statement about our essential human nature. We can be commanded not to kill because killing is not a necessary and unavoidable element of human nature. In the same way, people are innately able to avoid all forms of sin. Unless it is within our capacity, we would not have been commanded to be perfect.

This is not the same as claiming that people are naturally "good." People have free will, and being perfect requires freely choosing to follow the direction of the Light Within at all times and in all things. That may or may not result in doing what others might consider "good." What is essential is faithfulness.

Like salvation, perfection is not a state that is attained once and then continues effortlessly. It is a lifelong struggle to live up to the measure of Light we have received, always knowing that more can be asked of us. I think of it as acting your age. When you were two years old and acted in ways appropriate to that age, you were a perfect two-year-old. But, if you have continued to act in the same way, you are now far from being perfect.

Perfection is not necessary to be loved by God. Divine love is unconditional; God loves each of us as we are but yearns for us to grow into perfection and to continue to grow in perfection as long as we live.

Chapter 3
Changes in Quaker Faith and Practice over Time

The Light

Now with the light which is eternal, which searches, tries, examines, weighs, and makes all things manifest of what sort they are; let it search and try you, how you grow up in the eternal and immortal birth, and do not deceive your souls: For except you be born again, of water and of the spirit, ye cannot enter. Now see whether ye can read this in the light; and whether ye know, and see, and witness this in your own particulars, yea or nay.

Margaret Fell[1]

The Inward Light of Christ in the Seventeenth Century

The single most distinguishing attribute of the Religious Society of Friends since its inception has been the belief that everyone can be in direct, unmediated communication with the Inward Teacher and that, all by itself, this divine gift is sufficient to guide anyone to salvation. No subscription to a creed or a set of doctrines is required, nor is the performance of a set of rites and rituals. All other aspects of Quaker faith and practice grow out of this single principle "as the fingers shoot out of the hand."[2] This principle has many names, including that of God in each person, the Inward Light of Christ, the Inner Light, and the Light Within. Often today it is just called "the Light."

In the seventeenth century, this Light was identified with the Divine Light described in the first chapter of John's gospel. In the ninth verse, it says that this Light enlightens everyone who comes into the world. For early Quakers, this wasn't a metaphor. They believed the Inward Light to be real and originating in God. Although it may be understood by analogy to the light from the sun, it isn't by any means the same as natural light. Just as sunlight comes from the sun but is not the sun, this inwardly shining divine illumination is from God but is not God. We see things in the outside world because they are illuminated by the sun, and we see our inward spiritual world because it is illuminated by this Light shining into our hearts and our consciences.

Friends understood the Light Within to act primarily in three ways: searching and revealing, directing and guiding, and forgiving and empowering.

Searching and Revealing

This I told them was their first step to peace, even to stand still in the light that showed them their sins and transgressions.

George Fox[3]

The first motion of the Light Within is to reveal spiritual darkness, disclosing everything contrary to itself. It exposes good and evil, both in the world at large and within each individual. As a result, people can become aware of how and when they have fallen short. Unless we can distinguish right and wrong, we cannot be expected to choose one and reject the other. Until we realize that we have personally participated in sinful acts, we will have no reason to change our behavior and cannot be expected to do so. The Inward Light reveals all this. Thus, standing still in the Light and inwardly beholding whatever the Light uncovers is the first step towards reconciliation with God.

Directing and Guiding

Why shouldst thou sleep the Sleep of Death,
And lie in Sorrow down beneath,
When Light *is given thee for thy Guide,*
To bring thee from thy Life of Pride?

Ann Docwra[4]

No one is forced to pay attention to what the Light exposes. Just as we can close our outward, physical eyes to those things in the ordinary world that we find unpleasant and don't want to see, we have the ability to close our inward, spiritual eyes and turn away from what the Light of Christ reveals inside us. But knowing that evil is real and acknowledging the spiritual darkness within ourselves doesn't show us the way out. Knowing we need to change is not sufficient to compel change. Without guidance, we could just flail about, trying one thing after another without improving our circumstances. The Light Within reveals the divine will—what the All-Merciful One hopes and desires for us. Beyond illuminating that goal, it makes visible the spiritual path we need to walk in order to get there. And when we inevitably stray from that path, it shows us how to find our way back to it. The second action of the Inward Light is to point the way to reconciliation with God.

Forgiving and Empowering

Stand still in that which is pure, after ye see yourselves; and then mercy comes in. After thou seest thy thoughts, and the temptations, do not think, but submit; and then power comes. Stand still in that which shows and discovers; and there doth

> *strength immediately come. And stand still in the light, and submit to it, and the other will be hushed and gone; and then content comes.*
>
> George Fox[5]

If we had to depend on our own resources, seeing our true conditions and knowing what an Infinitely Compassionate Being hopes for us could lead only to guilt and spiritual paralysis. The task can feel overwhelming and our own abilities inadequate, but we are not alone. If we let it, the Inward Light empowers us. It reveals our Sustainer's love for us and God's depth of willingness to forgive our past mistakes. This in turn empowers us to resist evil—to walk in the Light—and, when we falter, it bolsters us.

The Light Within provides each of us with a sufficient measure of strength to cast off the dark ways in which we have been living and to follow the path of authentic living we have been shown. As an individual grows in faithfulness, more Light is granted and more is expected of him or her. Reconciliation with God is not a one-time event but an ongoing, lifelong process.

Knowing God

> *[God] is the light – and extends beams of his light to the eye of our souls or minds, as the outward light, the sun, does to the eye of our bodies. Hereby we may receive the manifestation and knowledge of God, and that too by his own light.*
>
> *As we cannot know the sun, but by its own light and influence, no more can we know God, but by his own immediate light and influence.*
>
> Job Scott[6]

Chapter 3: Changes in Quaker Faith and Practice over Time

This short sketch of how the Light works within each person discloses more than the nature and actions of the Spiritual Light. It also reveals early Friends' understanding of human nature and the purpose of our lives. Left to our own devices, we are weak and selfish. When we separate ourselves from the Inward Light, we are secretive—hiding even from ourselves—prone to sin, directionless and vulnerable. When we open our inward eyes to the Light, we are empowered to fulfill the purpose of our lives—to acknowledge and overcome our limitations and to live faithfully.

Spiritual illumination does more than just reveal darkness. It also grants each person an immediate experience of God. This unmediated access was one of the touchstones of seventeenth-century Quakerism. Those attending either an Anglican or a Puritan worship service heard a sermon *about* God from a priest or minister, but Friends claimed to hear the voice of God and to know the Inward Teacher directly.

The Analogy to Natural Light

Sing and rejoice, ye children of the day and of the light; for the Lord is at work in this thick night of darkness that may be felt.
George Fox[7]

Prior to the scientific exploration of the properties of light during the Enlightenment, the common understandings of natural light and natural darkness were very different from what we know today. People viewed each as having its own substance; they understood light as a thing and darkness as an opposing material. There is ancient evidence of this way of thinking in Genesis 1:4, in which the Creator needs to devote a period of time and effort on the first day of creation to separate darkness from light.

By the terms of this proposition, darkness resists light. When you lit a candle, it was assumed that the light radiating from the flame had to push against the darkness in order to clear out a small lighted space. If you needed to illuminate more space, you might use an oil lamp. Lamplight was brighter and therefore able to push the darkness farther back, carving out a larger sphere of radiance. The brighter the light source, the more darkness it was able to overcome.

Moreover, just as there are bright lights and dim lights, there are degrees of darkness. In 1663, George Fox was imprisoned in a cell that admitted no light—a chamber crammed with utter blackness. He opened an epistle to Friends with the words above that reflected the visceral nature of this darkness: "darkness that may be felt." He felt himself enfolded in a dense outward darkness.

When a common word is used as analogous to a spiritual reality, people naturally carry along the ordinary characteristics associated with the word in understanding its spiritual meaning. What this meant in the seventeenth century was that, like natural light and dark, Spiritual Light and Spiritual Darkness were implicitly assumed to have separate and opposing substances. They existed in an analogous state of mutual confrontation. Both were real, with the Inward Light originating in God and Spiritual Darkness in opposition to God. People recognized Darkness as sin and evil, the products of Satan. Just as they believed they could see night's darkness actively limiting the scope of a candle's light, they also believed they could see Spiritual Darkness actively opposing Spiritual Light and working to constrain its extent. This is announced explicitly in John 1:5: "And the light shineth in darkness; and the darkness comprehended it not" (here 'comprehend' means 'seize,' 'hold,' or 'entrap').

Chapter 3: Changes in Quaker Faith and Practice over Time

George Fox likewise referred to the physical nature of darkness in his *Journal* when he wrote, "I saw also, that there was an ocean of darkness and death; but an infinite ocean of light and love, which flowed over the ocean of darkness."[8] Spiritual darkness is real and resilient—strong enough to drown the unaided—but not strong enough to resist the Inward Light of Christ.

The Analogy Today

Just as part of early Friends' understanding of Spiritual Light came by analogy to natural light, so does ours today. However, the ways we commonly think about natural light isn't the same. Centuries of scientific exploration into the properties of light have changed how it is characterized and, consequently, how people conceive it. Natural light is composed of a stream of physical photons—each one has mass and substance. But darkness has no material substance; it is merely the absence of light. Since darkness is insubstantial, it has no ability to resist light.

When we flip a switch, a room is lighted—the dark doesn't have to be swept away; it simply ceases. A candle may be no brighter than it was four hundred years ago, but we know that the photons it emits can travel just as far and just as fast as those from the brightest laser. The darkness of outer space is powerless in the presence of photons streaming from a star billions of light-years away. A distant star is not dimmer because there is darkness holding its photons back. Interstellar dust or cosmic bodies may block the way, but the star appears dimmer primarily because the same number of photons spread out to fill a larger and larger volume of space as they travel farther and farther from their source.

This transformation in the scientific descriptions of natural light and darkness has profoundly changed Friends' perception of

Spiritual Light and, even more, their experience of Spiritual Darkness. Just as natural darkness has no material existence and is inexorably dispelled by light, Quakers now seem to think of Spiritual Darkness as simply an emptiness—as an absence of goodness. More importantly, darkness is no longer felt to be an embodiment of evil. Thus, Spiritual Darkness is not an active, wicked force. It has no ability to resist or constrain the Light Within.

Another subtle shift in our relationship with natural light plays out in the way we relate to Spiritual Light. In the seventeenth century, the main source of light was from the sun—a source that people had no control over. The darkness of night could be overcome to a very limited degree with fire. People could set big fires outside on the ground, smaller fires in a fireplace, and torches and little fires in lamps or on the tips of candles. Humanity had limited ability to determine what would be illuminated. Starting a fire from cold materials was not simple; easily lit matches were not invented until the nineteenth century. By contrast, today we can light up an enormous space at the flip of a switch. Light has become just one more mechanical servant at our command.

Our language about Spiritual Light demonstrates how very differently we think of it. For early Friends, it took courage to stand still in the Light—the Light of Christ Within threatened to discover and reveal things hidden within our hearts that we would prefer to hide and ignore. It was dangerous to see ourselves truthfully because it meant being spiritually exposed—stripped naked before the All-Seeing One. The Light challenged early Quakers to relinquish their self-image and their self-importance and to change, to repent, to be transformed. Under our modern understanding of darkness, however, standing still in the Light promises to painlessly brush away any darkness. Today, in fact, the Inner Light is more than just harmless; it's pleasantly warming and comforting.

Rather than standing still in the Light of Christ and allowing it to expose us, we have assumed the power to direct the Light as we see fit. When we say we will hold someone in the Light, it is as if we had the power to flip a spiritual switch, directing a benevolent Inner Light to shine forth on our designated recipient.

From Inward to Inner

It should also be noted that the choice of terms to use to describe the Light has changed over time. The Light was frequently referred to as the 'Inward Light' in the Society's first two hundred years. After about 1850, the incidence of that term gradually declined. On the other hand, prior to the first quarter of the nineteenth century, the term 'Inner Light' was rare in Quaker writing. Over the next century, that term steadily increased in use. Although these two terms may be seen as synonymous, there is a subtle difference between them. Movement is implied by 'inward.' It holds the sense of something that is directed from the outside to the inside. The Inward Light designates a portion of a single spiritual element that originates in God and travels into every person's heart and soul. 'Inner' does not carry the same implication. An Inner Light is more contained. It is easier to think of it as a separate spark of light residing within each individual.

The Inner Light in the Twenty-First Century

It is quite difficult to describe what the Inner Light means to contemporary Friends. The term is broadly used in so many different ways by the different types of Quakers and in such a variety of ways within each of our branches that there can be no single definition. For some Friends, it has been subsumed entirely into other Christian categories, becoming no more than a synonym for the Holy Spirit or for divine love and grace. Others speak of the Light as if it were a human faculty, perhaps just another name for the conscience. The older sense of the Inward Light as "not of us but of God" has been lost and is reduced to "this little light of mine." The older sense of a powerful searchlight probing the depths of our hearts and piercing our souls is almost entirely gone.

I attended a Catholic grade school, and most of my teachers were loving, good-hearted nuns. They refuted the stereotype of a nun as an overbearing, hardline disciplinarian. The theology they passed on to us (at least as we children were able to understand it) was actually quite simple: "God is love, and he's watching you all the time." This combination of love and surveillance was personified in our personal guardian angels. There was one assigned to each of us. Somehow, I got the idea that I could send my guardian angel on spiritual missions. Now and then, I sent my guardian angel to visit and comfort sick people in the hospital (I thought this would score me extra points I might need for the last judgment). Sometimes, when I hear Friends talk about the Light, I am reminded of those angelic missions.

This modern Light isn't in the least bit frightening; it does not threaten to unveil our innermost secrets. It's a heat lamp for the soul—soothing and comforting, protecting and healing. This Light brings spiritual relief and eases us into well-being. Rather than directing us, we direct it, identifying those in need and sending a packet of Inner Light to the rescue.

Such a view of the Light carries implications for how we view human nature and what we are to achieve in life. It assumes people are naturally good but vulnerable and frequently wounded. Our purpose in life is to be happy and to make others happy—to fulfill our hopes and dreams.

Chapter 3: Changes in Quaker Faith and Practice over Time

Quaker Christianity

NOW everlasting happiness and salvation depends upon true Christianity. Not upon having the name of a Christian only, or professing such or such Christian doctrines; but upon having the nature of Christianity, upon being renewed by the Spirit of Christ, and receiving the Spirit, walking in the Spirit, and bringing forth the fruits of the Spirit.

Isaac Penington[9]

Quaker Christianity in the Seventeenth Century

The first Friends were unequivocally Christian, and they knew what that meant. When George Fox said "Jesus Christ is come to teach his people, and to bring them from all the world's ways to Christ the way, the truth, and the life,"[10] he was referring to the Gospel of John (14:6) as well as proclaiming a new and different relationship between the Creator, human creatures, and the whole of creation. This was a Christian statement, but it wasn't one premised on anyone else's definition of what it meant to be a Christian. Early Friends didn't accept others' creeds as descriptive of true Christianity. Instead, they defined what it meant to be a true Christian from their own experience and lived according to that definition.

It would have been far easier to acquiesce to an Anglican or Puritan definition of Christianity. Early Quakers loudly declared not only that they were Christian but also that only they knew what was essential to being a Christian—living in faithful obedience to the guidance of the Inward Light of Christ. They embraced 1 Peter 2:9, "But ye are a chosen generation, a royal priesthood, an holy nation, a peculiar people; that ye should shew forth the praises of him who hath called you out of darkness into his marvellous light," as applying to them. They were God's chosen people.

The Orthodoxy of Early Quaker Beliefs

> *AND lest any should say we are Equivocal in our Expressions, and Allegorize away Christ's Appearance in the Flesh . . . [Friends believe in] his Coming, Birth, Miracles, Sufferings, Death, Resurrection, Ascension, Mediation and Judgment . . . That he was born of the Virgin Mary, Suffered under Pontius Pilate, the Roman Governor, was Crucified, Dead, and Buried in the Sepuchre of Joseph of Arimathea; Rose again the Third Day, and Ascended into Heaven, and sits on the Right Hand of God, in the Power and Majesty of his Father.*
>
> William Penn[11]

The Children of the Light, like Quakers today, did not have a creed, i.e., a formal statement of beliefs that delineated what it meant to be a Christian. Like the early Christians, they held a variety of beliefs. If they were asked, William Penn's statement (above) would have been accepted without question by most, if not all, of his fellow worshippers. In this respect they were orthodox in their faith, but to them this was not the whole of what it meant to be a Christian.

Why Were Friends Persecuted?

If Quakers were similar to other Protestants of their day in so many ways, why, then, were they persistently persecuted?

In part, it was simply because they defied English law by not participating in the official national church. It was commonly held in Europe at the time that church and state were properly and

Chapter 3: Changes in Quaker Faith and Practice over Time

necessarily interlocked. The head of the Church of England was the king or queen. Likewise, under the Commonwealth, Parliament exercised ecclesiastical authority. It was widely assumed that national unity and civil security required religious unity. Anyone who rejected the established church implicitly challenged political authority. Quakers were persecuted for not being Puritan during the Commonwealth and for not being Anglican following the restoration of Charles II.

As is so often the case, money was also involved. Not only did Friends refuse to worship in the legally stipulated manner, they also refused government-enforced demands for the payment of church tithes, a tax levied to support the religious establishment. Their actions were an invitation to fines and imprisonment, and that is exactly what they got. The resulting persecution was sufficiently severe that London Yearly Meeting established a Meeting for Sufferings in 1668 to help the many thousands of Quakers and their families who suffered outwardly for being faithful.

More fundamentally, both the established church and other Protestant sects professed to be Christians, but, in Quaker eyes, they did not possess the truth of Christianity in their hearts. As George Fox wrote in 1657, "ye profess what you do not possess."[12] In other words, Friends were true Christians; all others only pretended to be. Others may have faithfully followed the prescribed outward rites and rituals, but Friends knew Christ inwardly.

The standing of Scripture also distinguished Friends from other Protestants. The Quaker trust in the Inward Light of Christ and their maintaining it as the ultimate rule and guide to life—that the Light had greater authority in that respect than the Bible—was viewed as heretical. Quakers believed the Bible is the ultimate *outward* guide to right living but assigned it a secondary position.

The Scriptures, they said, were not "the Word of God" but words of God—and Friends heard additional divine words.

In his *Apology*, Robert Barclay described the Spirit of God as "the fountain of all truth and right reason" and declared it the ultimate source of inspiration for the Bible's writers. While the scriptures are a beneficial guide, "Nevertheless, because they are only a declaration of the fountain, and not the fountain itself, therefore they are not to be esteemed the principal ground of all truth and knowledge, nor yet the adequate primary rule of faith and manners."[13] In short, the Bible is subordinate to directly experienced divine revelations. Moreover, Friends were advised to read scripture solely under the guidance of the Spirit of God—not under the guidance of any human, no matter how well educated. To other Protestants, this was anathema.

Finally, the early Friends declared the Light Within to be both necessary and sufficient for anyone to attain salvation. Quakers asserted it was possible for any individual to be saved merely by faithfully attending to the guidance of the Inward Light. Being a Christian was unnecessary; knowledge of Jesus or the Bible was not needed. Indeed, they explicitly included Jews and Muslims among those who could be saved in this way, thereby embracing two groups of people who would know of Jesus but who rejected Christian claims about him. Jews (especially those living in a Christian country) would know who Jesus was—a first-century Jew but not the promised Messiah and certainly not divine. In the Qur'an, Muslims found Jesus celebrated as the greatest prophet prior to Muhammed, but Jesus was a human prophet only, not "the Son of God." In short, both "Turk and Jew" explicitly denied the divinity of Christ, and yet the Quakers said Muslims and Jews could be saved.

Chapter 3: Changes in Quaker Faith and Practice over Time

In 1689, Parliament passed the Act of Toleration. This enacted into law exactly what it says: toleration, not acceptance. None of the laws that had been enacted to persecute Friends were repealed, but now they would no longer be enforced. Quakers would be endured, not embraced. In return, they were expected to accept the proposition that they were but a small part of the body of Christ— a fragment of a much larger church. Many Friends accommodated themselves to the broader English religious culture, but others resisted and continued to claim that their unique understanding of Christianity was the only true one.

The One True Church

The Humble, Meek, Merciful, Just, Pious *and* Devout Souls, *are every where of one Religion; and when Death has taken off the Mask, they will know one another, though the diverse Liveries they wear here, make them Strangers.*
                                                        William Penn[14]

Early Friends asserted that they were the only true Christians. They claimed to have stripped away centuries of add-ons and restored the purity of the church as it existed in the days of the apostles. Even so, they did not promise a beeline to heaven for those who joined with them. Just being Quaker was not enough. Salvation was understood to be an ongoing job. Each person needed to strive for perfection every day. The activity of the Light Within was sufficient to show people where to go and to provide the strength needed to walk that path, but it was up to each person to freely choose to follow that guidance and to set his or her feet on that course. If they did not, they were not saved and had no one to blame but themselves.

As mentioned above, those who were not Friends were by no means precluded from entering that spiritual paradise. The Inward Light of Christ shines into everyone and is alone sufficient to guide and empower each person to live faithfully and to find their way to whatever afterlife might be awaiting. Being saved requires living faithfully, not endorsing the right creed, reading the right book, or practicing the right rituals. Even believing in God is not necessary if a person follows the guidance of the Inward Teacher.

In short, although primitive Friends declared that they were the only true Christians, they did not claim to be the only members of the one true church. Those would only be revealed "when Death has taken off the Mask."

Quaker Christianity in the Twenty-First Century

The fractured history of the Religious Society of Friends in the last three and a half centuries has resulted in several distinct dialects of Quaker Christianity. These cross the spectrum from Evangelical to liberal. Some call themselves Christian Quakers; others shift the emphasis by declaring themselves Quaker Christians; still others reject the label "Quaker" entirely, describing themselves as Christian and members of the Friends Church.

Quaker beliefs regarding Jesus are correspondingly varied. To some, he is an important ethical teacher but not divine. Other Friends find this description not only inadequate but insulting to the Divine Redeemer and Savior of the World. The diversity of Christian beliefs found among Friends today is greater than at any earlier time, and I will not attempt to catalogue them all nor pretend I could single one out as the right one.

Primitive Quakers were steeped in Scripture. Besides seeing it as a storehouse of divine revelation, they engaged the Bible as a source of preserved ancient wisdom. That is as true now as it was

Chapter 3: Changes in Quaker Faith and Practice over Time

then, and the ongoing work of biblical scholars to better understand the origins and original meanings of these inspired writings has added to our knowledge. Our forebears claimed the responsibility to interpret those stories and poems and other narratives under the direction of the Holy Spirit. That is our heritage, and it is worth claiming.

Today, too many Friends have given up on their unique Christian heritage and accepted others' definitions of Christianity as true, whether it is one with which they agree or not. Some are uncomfortable with a particular form of Christianity they knew as a child or at some other point in their lives that they have since rejected. Although it may be an accurate description (or a caricature) of one particular expression of the Christian message, they have somehow come to assume it is the only "official" definition. Since they find that definition unacceptable, they declare themselves "not Christian." In doing so, that they have ceded authority to someone else's definition instead of expressing—as our spiritual forebears did—a Quaker form of Christianity.

Early Friends too encountered forms of Christianity that they considered wrongheaded. Rather than relinquishing their birthright to be called Christians, they proudly claimed the title for themselves. They insisted on their own definition of what that really meant—even to the extent of labeling their opponents as "so-called" or "pretended" Christians. While it isn't necessary to insult others, we would individually and as the Society of Friends greatly benefit from the work of exploring and expressing what it means to be Quaker and Christian today.

Meeting for Worship

Ironically for a society founded in part on the idea that outward forms are not essential, some Friends today identify Quakerism with an outward form of worship. Those who follow a different order of worship are too often pronounced "not really Friends." Within many of our congregations, we willingly accept multitudes of theological variation with equanimity and forbearance, but we do not accept a single change in our Sunday morning routine. I have heard unprogrammed worship described as boring and prepared sermons as contrived. But my experience is that all Quakers are experimental in their approach to worship. We mix and match—and complain about changes.

My preferred form of worship is unstructured and untimed, guided only by the immediate direction of the Holy Spirit. I have spent hours in profound silence punctuated by occasional prayers, singing, and heartfelt messages. I have felt the movement of the Unutterable and the Divine dancing among those gathered. I have felt that same movement in a Hispanic Evangelical Friends church and in a calm period of expectant waiting following a prepared sermon. I have also felt my heart jangled and contentious as I searched for composure among a stilled body of Friends.

To be clear, on occasion I have been asked to "bring the message," that is, to come to a programmed meeting with a prepared sermon, and I have also served as interim pastor in a Friends church. None of those experiences has led me to abandon my precious times of unprogrammed worship.

Worship in the Seventeenth Century

> *OH! how sweet and pleasant is it to the truly spiritual eye, to see several sorts of believers, several forms of Christians in the*

Chapter 3: Changes in Quaker Faith and Practice over Time

> *school of Christ, every one learning their own lesson, performing their own peculiar service, and knowing, owning, and loving one another in their several places, and different performances to their Master, to whom they are to give an account, and not to quarrel one with another about their different practices! This is the true ground of love and unity, not that such a man walks and does just as I do, but because I feel the same Spirit of life in him, and that he walks in his rank, in his own order, in his proper way and place of subjection to that.*
>
> Isaac Penington[15]

Opportunities to worship in community were frequent in our earliest days. The earliest Friends met together on Sunday morning, again on Sunday afternoon, and still again for a midweek meeting on Wednesday or Thursday. Each meeting for worship could last for three hours or more. The "order of service" was simple. Friends gathered at an appointed hour and sat together in silence. Children stayed the entire time, usually sitting with their mothers. Those who had been recognized as elders or ministers often sat on a designated "facing" bench (so called because it faced towards the reset of the congregation). In some places, this was elevated to allow the elders a ready view of the gathered congregation and so a minister's voice would more easily carry to the back benches and be heard by all.

At most meetings for worship, one or more of those present offered ministry or prayer, and it was not uncommon for an individual, particularly a visiting minister, to speak for an hour or longer. These sermons were not prepared in advance but were composed and delivered on the spot under the direct inspiration of the Holy Spirit. Some of those who spoke would say that they had been an instrument in the divine hand—that is, that they had no more claim to the words they uttered than a flute could take credit for the music played on it. Although much of the ministry was offered by those recognized as ministers, all were free to speak if they felt divinely inspired. Anyone—man or woman, rich or poor—who spoke well over a period of time might be asked to assume the role of a recognized minister and move to the facing bench.

The content of vocal ministry in earlier centuries can only be guessed at. Since it was unplanned, no sermon notes are available. Likewise, only on rare occasions would the content of vocal ministry be recorded or be discussed in other Quaker writings. Even so, we can be sure that the Bible shaped much of its content. Many of these Friends knew large tracts of Scripture by heart, and their ministry undoubtedly was inspired by it and was saturated with phrases, allusions, and references to those sacred writings. Early Quakers did not, however, bring their Bibles into the meeting or have formal Scripture readings. That would have been stealing words that had been given to another rather than restricting themselves to those utterances that had been given to a speaker in the course of the meeting for worship.

In our earliest times, hymns and psalms were spontaneously sung in the course of ministry, but the congregation was unlikely to have joined in singing. The words that had been given to one member of the congregation were hers or his alone to offer. For someone else to sing them would have been "out of the Spirit."

Changes over the Centuries

Some early Friends took the admonishment to do no advance planning to extremes. They insisted that God's chosen people would be divinely gathered together at the right time and in the right place and that there was therefore no need to set a meeting

Chapter 3: Changes in Quaker Faith and Practice over Time

time or place. This experiment failed, and with it went the pure ideal of worship in spirit and truth. Some prearrangement is necessary. Exactly how much and which elements of worship should be planned have been points of ongoing contention and shifting boundaries over the ensuing centuries. This has resulted in the varieties of worship found among Friends today.

The length and frequency of meetings for worship have steadily declined over the last three hundred and fifty years. Untimed meetings lasting three hours or longer shrank to two hours and then one hour. Some meetings for worship today are even shorter. Attendance at a second meeting for worship on Sunday evening diminished to the point where it has almost entirely disappeared. Some meetings continue to hold a midweek worship, but this is rare. In parallel with the changed duration of meetings for worship, the length of individual sermons has decreased. Totally silent meetings became more frequent, although even in the Quietist[*] period in the eighteenth and early nineteenth centuries nearly all meetings for worship included some vocal ministry or prayer.

A number of formal styles of ministry have developed and disappeared. For a time, it was fashionable to begin ministry in a very low, almost inaudible voice and build in volume as the sermon progressed. Some speakers took exaggerated breaths, gasping for air between words or sobbing loudly and frequently. In later years,

---

[*] Quietism is a spiritual movement that arose in the Catholic Church in the seventeenth century and became influential among Quakers. Quietists question the spiritual value of anything that originates in their own minds. In prayer, they seek to become empty vessels—to quiet all thoughts, desires, hopes, dreams, ideas, and acts of will—in order to be as receptive as possible to the pure will of God. One effect of this on Friends was to lead them to rigorously examine any inclination to offer ministry during meetings for worship. As a result, the number of messages spoken declined dramatically.

a characteristic sing-song style became customary. Each time, the use of an exaggerated style grew over time until eventually, in the elders' opinion, style came to overshadow content in the ministry and they intervened.

Singing seems to have disappeared after the first few decades but has reappeared repeatedly, often as individual ministry arising from the stillness, sometimes joined by others in the congregation. Today, some Friends meetings and many Friends churches have choirs, and singing is a standard element in their order of worship. Even the Friends General Conference, which consists almost exclusively of meetings with unprogrammed meetings for worship, has published a hymnal.

In the first decades of the nineteenth century, Sunday Schools for adults and children spread in other Protestant churches, and a few Quaker meetings followed the example, establishing what they called First Day Schools. Hicksite meetings initially resisted this "innovation," but by 1900 it was nearly universal in all branches of the Society. As a result, most children stopped attending the entire period of worship.

Of course, the most noticeable changes in the form of worship took place among those Friends who adopted a set order of service with prewritten sermons, hymn singing, and preselected scripture readings—with or without a hired minister. The degree of programming varies widely, and in some cases these additions have nearly crowded out quietly waiting on the Holy Spirit. In most cases, however, Friends recognize that these doings are only aids, intended to help the congregation to prepare for, to benefit in the midst of, and then to return from a period of waiting for the immediate inspiration of the Holy Spirit. All the additions are merely the wrappings on the divine gift of free ministry.

Chapter 3: Changes in Quaker Faith and Practice over Time

Worship in the Twenty-First Century

Even the simplest period of worship can be the source of great unhappiness. Several years ago, my wife was asked to take responsibility for the early morning worship at a gathering of Friends, most from the unprogrammed tradition. Peggy thought it would be an agreeable and spiritually fulfilling assignment. On the first day, she arrived early to be sure the door was unlocked and an adequate number of chairs was set in a circle, and then she settled in the stillness while others arrived. Sometime later, she felt called to offer vocal ministry. After about an hour, she closed worship by shaking hands with those closest to her and got up to head for breakfast in the cafeteria. Before she reached the door, a distraught young man intercepted her, protesting that her speaking had intruded on his time of meditation. "It was *supposed* to be a *silent* worship," he insisted crossly.

It would be a mistake to think that so-called unprogrammed meetings have preserved the waiting worship of our spiritual ancestors without changes. The obvious differences in frequency and duration have profoundly altered the quality of worship. At least as important are the rules for speaking that are embedded in silent meetings for worship: don't speak too long or too early or too soon after another's offering, do not respond to another's ministry, etc.

There are also rituals wrapped around the worship period. Group singing before meeting is common. In some cases, this occurs in the meeting room and leads directly into the silence. Some meetings prepare for worship by holding a premeeting discussion on a predetermined topic. In others, a preprinted reading is distributed as people arrive. Preselected queries or "Quaker quotes" may be read aloud as the meeting settles.

At the close of worship, some meetings invite those present to share their "joys and concerns," which in other churches might be called prayer requests. This may be followed with a stock closing phrase such as, "Are all hearts clear?" Those in attendance may be asked if they wish to "share something that didn't rise to the level of ministry" or to "offer afterthoughts." After announcements, "Meeting may rise" is frequently heard. These are rituals that the elders of an earlier generation might have confronted.

Each of these changes arose for a reason. They were first introduced because someone believed they would enhance the quality of worship or strengthen the meeting community. Some were introduced into the Society of Friends by people who were raised in other religious traditions and who missed certain elements from the services of their youth; others are simply things we enjoy doing together. Some enrich and some interfere—often at the same time for different individuals in the same congregation. As Isaac Penington reminded us above, the purpose of a meeting for worship is not to worship in one form or another but to "feel the same Spirit of life." We have been gathered to bring us into communion with the Infinite Spirit and with each other. We must be willing to give up the things we do simply because we are used to doing them or because we enjoy them. At the same time, we need to be open to changes that lead us into deeper spiritual communion, greater love, and closer unity.

The ultimate criterion for any practice is whether it helps the worshippers meet the One Worshipped.

Speech

They recommended Silence by their Example, having very few Words upon all Occasions. . . . Nor could they humour the Custom of Good Night, Good Morrow, Good Speed; for they

Chapter 3: Changes in Quaker Faith and Practice over Time

knew the Night was Good, and the Day was Good, without wishing of either; and that in the other Expression, the Holy Name of God was too lightly and unthankfully used, and therefore taken in vain. Besides, they were Words and Wishes of Course, and are usually as little meant.

William Penn[16]

We use speech primarily to try to shape our public personas. Moreover, our choice of words reveals our hidden assumptions about the nature of reality, of God, and of our relationship with the Divine. How we address one another, what is acceptable and unacceptable in common discourse, and the standards for truth that we choose to uphold all reveal more than the surface language. For these reasons, and more, Friends have been cautioned to choose their words deliberately and intentionally for more than three hundred and fifty years.

Quaker Speech in the Seventeenth Century

Several elements of the unique Quaker dialect developed in the early years of the Society of Friends. While this section may appear to be a random collection of separate, individual practices, underlying each one was a call for radical truthfulness and uncompromising faithfulness in everything a person said.

Honors and Flattery

The best remembered bit of Quakerese is the use of the second-person-singular pronouns 'thou' and 'thee' and 'thy' and 'thine' when speaking to a single person. In the mid-seventeenth century, Standard English still employed different singular and plural forms of the second-person pronoun. As is still the case in many languages today, the convention of the time was to show respect to an individual by using the plural forms of address. This

77

most notably occurred when speaking with a person deemed to be a social superior. Thus, a commoner would address a member of the nobility as 'you' (plural form) but would use 'thou' (singular form) when speaking to another commoner. The noble would respond using 'thou' since the commoner was a social inferior and deserved no deference. Likewise, a parent might say 'thou' to a child, and the child might reply with 'you.' The use of honorifics, such as 'Your Majesty' for the king, 'Your Honor' for a judge, or 'Your Excellency' for a bishop, performed similar functions (notice that each of these uses the plural form 'your').

The plural forms were also sometimes used as a blatant form of flattery, offering false honor that social convention didn't demand. They were the kinds of "little white lies" that grease the skids of social interactions. To English commoners, such usages were considered polite and a sign of good manners, but to the Publishers of Truth, such marks of distinction offered unmerited honor and glory to a mere human creature. Fawning feeds self-importance, vanity, and arrogance—spiritually injuring the recipient. Even when it wasn't deliberate flattery, these practices fed the recipient's pride and were spiritually harmful.

In actively avoiding such practices, Quakers violated the norms of courteous social discourse. It is easy to see why Quakers were considered unnecessarily rude and disrespectful. Sometimes this witness was also dangerous. Not a few early Friends were struck with a cane for failing to use the expected pronoun. An incensed judge could jail an offender for failing to address the bench as "Your Honor."

It is important to remember that this was not just a private vernacular for the initiates to use with each other or a way to gain the attention of others. It was a public witness against pride and a testimony directed to the souls of others. The "plain speech" was

Chapter 3: Changes in Quaker Faith and Practice over Time

a plea for humility and repentance. It was an outward act of love for a damaged fellow creature. The early Friends did not reserve this language for use among themselves; it was part of their testimony to the world, and all were expected to witness to it at all times. Using 'thou' when addressing other Quakers but 'you' when greeting non-Friends was hypocritical and grounds for disciplinary action by one's meeting.

Although using the singular forms started out simply as a practice that Friends felt divinely obligated to follow, by the eighteenth century it had become a sectarian requirement. Failing to use the plain speech could result in a visit from the elders.

Names for Days and Months

The Friends of Truth followed the example of the Puritans and many other Protestant Reformers in referring to the days of the week and months of the year by their number (e.g., First Day and Second Month). The common names that had been given to some of the days and months honored pagan gods. For example, March is named for Mars, the Roman god of war, and Thursday for Thor, the Norse god of storms and thunder. Our spiritual ancestors felt they could not honor false gods even in this seemingly innocent way.

Greetings and Salutations

Greeting someone with the common salutations of the time also came under scrutiny. Just as Quakers did not greet others with a bow and the honorific "your humble servant," neither could they say, "How are you?" unless they were really inquiring about a person's health and were willing to devote the time needed to hear an honest answer. Similarly, since "goodbye" is a contraction of "God be with you," it was only to be used when one really wished to offer a blessing. Otherwise, as Penn put it, "the Holy Name of

God was too lightly and unthankfully used." Such expressions were merely "Words and Wishes of Course"; they were essentially meaningless and were said to be pleasant and inoffensive or to satisfy a social convention. Faithfulness required a choice of words that meant what was intended at all times, even in the most inconsequential exchanges.

Oaths

Friends have famously refused to swear oaths, and this is often attributed to a desire to always be truthful. Although this is true, the ban on oaths was originally rooted in the Bible. Jesus instructed his disciples to "swear not at all" (Matthew 5:34), and his brother later elaborated on this command in his epistle: "But above all things, my brethren, swear not, neither by heaven, neither by the earth, neither by any other oath: but let your yea be yea; and your nay, nay; lest ye fall into condemnation" (James 5:12). Refusing to swear an oath was a scriptural duty. Only in the late 1890s was the single standard of truth put forward as a basis for this testimony.

Radical Truthfulness

Beyond these specific instances, there was a broader and deeper expectation of integrity; Friends were expected to be truthful at all times. In the seventeenth century, this meant that such ordinary behaviors as haggling over prices in the marketplace came under scrutiny. As was discussed in the previous chapter, a Quaker merchant was obliged to state a fair price and refuse any alternative. For a Quaker buyer, faithfulness required offering fair payment and being willing to forgo the purchase. This was not a tactic to get the best of a deal; it was public advocacy for radical truthfulness.

The purpose of Quaker plain speech was to be rigorously honest in all aspects of language. Jargon, flowery expressions, or unfamiliar technical terminology were avoided because they could impede others' understanding of what was said. Exaggeration, sarcasm, and flippancy might mislead a listener. Worse, these were all often intended to show off the speaker's cleverness and thus to feed her or his own pride.

Few words and simple words were preferred.

A Mid-Course Correction

Each of the elements of traditional Quaker-speak was affected by changes in the English language and the wider society in subsequent years. Social differences still existed, but many of the markers of those distinctions disappeared, were modified, or became obscured. The expectation that people would use different second-person pronouns depending on social class or status (or a desire to flatter) had largely disappeared from everyday English by the middle of the eighteenth century. Whereas Friends had attempted to level social differences by denying special honors to some, the surrounding culture moved in the opposite direction, granting everyone the respect implied by the second-person plural. With this change in English culture, the underlying purpose of using "thee" evaporated. By hanging onto an outdated concept, what had been a courageous witness became a cute and harmless idiosyncrasy.

In part because Friends maintained their refusal to swear oaths, legal practice changed. In the United States, it is now nearly always possible to make an affirmation in courts and in other situations where an oath is normally expected—stipulating that what will be said is true and acknowledging that the penalties for perjury apply.

By the end of the nineteenth century, nearly all Friends had abandoned these linguistic practices, and the expectation to do so had been removed from most Quaker books of discipline. This coincided with a number of other changes in the Society of Friends in the course of an extensive reevaluation of Quaker behavioral expectations in the nineteenth century.

Quaker Speech Today

Quaker language has continued to evolve. Perhaps most notable is a change in another personal pronoun. Until the last few centuries, God was referred to as "he" or "him" and was implicitly male, even though, as a spirit, God has no gender. Many contemporary Quakers avoid nouns and pronouns for God that are either explicitly or implicitly male or seem to support a patriarchal view of God. To fill the void, there has been an infusion of gender-neutral and female alternative names that have enriched our vocabularies.

Likewise, most Friends now use customary greetings and farewells without qualms. A judge is addressed as "Your Honor" and a minister as "Reverend" without giving it a second thought. In everyday conversation, nearly all contemporary Quakers sound just like everyone else.

Reclaiming Our Heritage

In other ways, however, I fear modern Quakers have allowed our language to atrophy. For a variety of reasons, some words have been dropped from everyday use without replacement. Much of this comes from an aversion to words that are uncomfortably associated with other denominations or theological positions. Words such as 'sin' and 'salvation' come to mind. In some cases, this has led to certain remaining words being overloaded with a multiplicity of meanings. In particular, 'Light' has been used in a many ways that would not be immediately understood by early Friends. New meanings include its use as a synonym for 'God' or for 'grace.' The result is that a seemingly simple phrase, such as "I will hold you in the Light," can mean very different things to different people; saying it does not necessarily convey a specific meaning.

Perhaps as important, by intentionally drawing from a broader vocabulary, we may be able to communicate more clearly and more easily with those who don't know our secret codes. Most Sunday morning visitors would immediately understand what it means to ask for prayers for a sick uncle and use that information to understand what is meant when someone asks that a troubled child be held in the Light. We don't have to give up words or phrases that have special meanings for Friends in order to reintegrate some of the traditional words Quakers once used into our vocabularies or to continue to assimilate new words as they come along. At the same time, recovering the traditional Quaker meanings of these words would give us a better understanding of our own heritage.

As discussed above, for a long time Friends have defined Christianity differently than their neighbors. Finding definitions that are uniquely and accurately our own would help others to identify our place in the religious landscape of the twenty-first century. You may not agree with previous definitions or with each other—just as you may not agree with definitions provided by other contemporary Christians—but working through what it means for you can deepen your spiritual life, even if your conclusion is that you are not a Christian.

Avoiding Discomfort

Some Friends feel that others try to control conversations and even vocal ministry by restricting the words they will allow to be used to describe spiritual experiences. I remember talking separately with two members of a meeting in a suburb of Chicago in the course of a few minutes. The first Friend told me that he felt censored—that he had been forbidden to use the Christian vocabulary he was comfortable with when speaking in meeting. Less than five minutes later, I was approached by another member who complained that she felt oppressed by what she described as the incessant and insistent use of Christian language during meeting for worship. Both were sincere, and both felt marginalized. They were estranged from each other, a state that could not help but tear at the fabric of their community.

I have in the past (and probably in those two conversations) urged "listening in tongues," i.e., internally translating "foreign" expressions into those words or phrases we would use ourselves. This may be a good way to overcome our immediate resistance and may preserve the peace within the meeting, but it comes at the cost of people talking past each other. It also values our own personal comfort above communication with others.

What I believe we are called to do is harder—not to translate but to listen to the words as they are spoken and to strive to understand the meanings they have for the person speaking them. That is, don't translate difficult words—grapple with them. When we do that, it opens us up and invites others to engage with us. We might have to check our perceptions by saying something like, "I want to be sure I understand you. Here's what that word means to me . . ." This can be a starting point for genuine dialogue.

If we cannot do that with people in our meetings, how can we hope to truly listen to and connect with those from outside the Society of Friends when a visitor shows up at our doors?

Inconsistencies

In responding to the changes in the surrounding culture, many Friends have become inconsistent in their forms of speech. Two examples stand out:

Chapter 3: Changes in Quaker Faith and Practice over Time

Nearly all Quakers have followed the rest of the culture and dropped the singular second-person pronouns from their vocabulary, but some Friends hold on to the original practice, feeling obliged to use 'thee' or 'thou' whenever addressing a single individual. Others use these terms, but not consistently. They reserve 'thee' and 'thou' for speaking with other Quakers or with family members but switch to Standard English when addressing others. In doing so, the tradition has been turned on its head. A practice originally intended to challenge and eliminate distinctions between people has itself become a way to distinguish those within the Religious Society of Friends from those on the outside.

Likewise, using numbers to refer to the days of the week and months of the year has developed into an isolating tradition lacking a theological or spiritual basis. Unless speaking to other Quakers, only a very few would set a meeting for Third Day afternoon or arrange a visit in the Ninth Month. Nor are we particularly conscientious in avoiding names that honor pagan gods. For example, the planets and many other bodies in the solar system are named for Roman gods, but we have not taken to calling them First Planet, Second Planet, etc.

This is a long way from holding to a single standard of truth.

New Traditions

At the same time, Friends have long been adding new idiosyncratic phrases to their distinctive in-group vernacular. Some expressions that we think date back to the first Friends are actually much more recent inventions. Here are a couple of examples:

- To "hold someone in the Light" never occurs in the writings of early Quakers and seems to have been created in the late twentieth century by Friends for whom the phrase "I'll pray for you" was uncomfortable. This neologism depends on an image of light as warm and nurturing—very different from the searching and discovering Light of Christ Within.

- Describing the meeting for business as "meeting for worship with a concern for business" was most likely first used in the 1970s or 1980s. The intent is to remind ourselves to seek the will of God in our business meetings. Although the use of the term may have a short-term effect, it violates the early Friends injunction to "let your words be few." In the meetings where I have heard it, many of those in the business meetings believe it is an ancient and traditional name rather than an invented tradition.

What needs to be asked is whether these kinds of new phrases are of value or are obstacles to clear communication. To me, they seem to be no more than likable catchphrases without essential content. Moreover, they can make newcomers feel excluded. Rather than facilitating the exchange of ideas, they can interfere when someone from outside the Society of Friends seeks to understand us.

Ultimately, do they advance a standard of radical truthfulness?

Relations with Earthly Governments

My Heart hath often been deeply afflicted under a Feeling I have had, that the Standard of pure Righteousness is not lifted up to the People by us, as a Society. . . . Friends being active in civil Society, in putting Laws in force which are not agreeable to the Purity of Righteousness, hath, for several Years, been an increasing Burthen upon me; having felt, in the Openings of universal Love, that where a People, convinced of the Truth of the inward Teachings of Christ, are active in putting Laws in Execution which are not consistent

Chapter 3: Changes in Quaker Faith and Practice over Time

with pure Wisdom, it hath a necessary Tendency to bring Dimness over their Minds.

John Woolman [17]

Different forms of government embody various ways for people to organize and regulate their relationships with each other. Successful ones provide collective services and a degree of physical security that could not be achieved by families or clans alone. In exchange, they demand people's allegiance and a share in what they produce. One nearly universal feature of human regimes is that they claim the exclusive right to the use of some forms of violence and coercion. Some of these forms are large-scale and externally applied, such as when resisting encroachment by other governments. Others are internal, such as employing a police force to control crime and a penal system to punish offenders. Coercion is inherent in this; you must do what the government says or it will resort to violence. The use of force may be considered legitimate and in the best interests of those who are governed, but some governments systematically use threats, intimidation, and force to suppress their own people or to impose their will on other groups of people. Ultimately, if it feels its continued existence is endangered, nearly every government will use armed force for self-preservation—even against its own citizenry.

Building a covenant community (or, to use the traditional term, the kingdom of heaven on earth) requires the willingness to confront human governments with a radical alternative—one with a spiritual foundation. That is what John Woolman and many other Quakers have called on the Religious Society of Friends to model. In the beloved community, our first and essential allegiance is to God, not to any human organization or political philosophy. For three hundred and fifty years, our calling as a people has been to practice this mode of living and to invite others to join in.

In the Seventeenth Century

Friends have had a difficult time finding the right relationship with governments since their earliest days. The Lamb's War was explicitly a confrontation with civil as well as religious authorities. The primitive Quakers were not, however, completely estranged from government. George Fox, for example, met in person with Oliver Cromwell several times when he held supreme authority as Lord Protector of the English Commonwealth. The famous 1660 "peace testimony" was a political document, written to convince King Charles II that Friends were loyal subjects of the crown and not a threat to the royal government.

Even more obvious were the roles of William Penn. Much of his time was spent in what we would now call lobbying. He achieved some success, but it came with a price. When King Charles II granted Penn a very large land grant in North America, it provided a haven for Quakers and other persecuted religious dissenters from England and elsewhere in Europe, but in accepting the province of Pennsylvania, Penn became its governor and therefore a vassal of the king. He was therefore part of the government that was actively persecuting his fellow Quakers. As the proprietor of the province, he set himself up to serve two masters: God and the king.

Penn was a member of the royal court, which gave him unique opportunities to advocate for religious tolerance. When James II ascended to the throne, Penn's position was enhanced because he was among the king's closest advisors on a broad range of matters. This relationship may have benefited the Society of Friends, but it so compromised Penn that, when James was overthrown in the

Chapter 3: Changes in Quaker Faith and Practice over Time

Glorious Revolution of 1688, Penn was assumed to be plotting against the new rulers. As a result, he was temporarily stripped of Pennsylvania and spent several years in hiding.

Changes over the Centuries

It was not until the nineteenth century that Quakers gained full religious and civil freedom in Great Britain and with it the right to hold office. A small but steady stream of British Friends has served in political offices ever since—some with distinction.

The course of events was very different in Britain's American colonies and later in the new United States. Quakers founded and directly controlled two colonies, West Jersey and Pennsylvania. In the early eighteenth century they also gained significant political power in two more provinces, Rhode Island and North Carolina. So long as these settlements remained isolated from the struggles between European monarchies and from frontier clashes with the Native Americans, holding office was not seen as being in conflict with Friends principles.

French and Indian War

That situation changed dramatically in the mid-1750s when Great Britain and France fought the Seven Years' War. Imperial hostilities spread to North America, where it was known as the French and Indian War. This led to frequent skirmishes and battles between European settlers and Native Americans. Regular army units and provincial militias were called out to protect colonists on the frontier. Royal demands that the colonial assemblies enact taxes to fund these actions directly entangled Quaker provincial officials in the war. It became clear that their responsibilities to the king and their religious duties were in fundamental conflict, and eventually most Friends withdrew from government service.

In 1762, Philadelphia Yearly Meeting approved a minute stating: "Liberty of conscience being ... essential to the well-being of religious societies, we ... therefore advise and exhort all in profession with us, to decline the acceptance of any office or station in civil government, the duties of which are inconsistent with our religious principles." The other North American yearly meetings soon followed suit. In some books of discipline, a list of specific offices was appended to the general prohibition, listing positions ranging from provincial (or state and federal) legislatures to the local justice of the peace. If a Quaker held a job in the government, she or he was to be "labored with" and, if he or she was unwilling to resign from civil service, disowned. This prohibition applied not just to officeholders. Philadelphia Yearly Meeting went on to say, "Friends ought not, in any wise, to be active or accessory in electing their brethren to such offices."[18] In other words, Friends were explicitly banned from supporting or voting for any office seeker, whether or not the candidate was a Quaker.

This proscription of political activity may sound bizarre to many twenty-first-century readers. They may wonder why all political action or government service was forbidden. Even if it seemed necessary to withdraw from government service, why was voting barred? The answer lies in the function of elections in a democracy. Voting is an implicit contract between the citizenry and the government. By voting, each voter legitimizes the winners' claims to govern in her or his name. By participating in the election, even those who did not support the victors are granting them the right to act as their agent. This entangles every voter in all subsequent actions of the resulting government. When blood is spilled or coercion used to achieve a government's goal, each voter deserves a share of the guilt. Eighteenth-century Friends believed

Chapter 3: Changes in Quaker Faith and Practice over Time

that we are a people chosen by God to model a different way—to live as an example of the peaceable kingdom. In their eyes, this required renunciation of public service, politicking, and voting.

Abolition

This withdrawal did not mean that Friends forfeited their right to petition their governments. They had opinions on public affairs and expressed them to their elected officials. Most notably in the United States, they consistently lobbied their state and federal governments to end slavery.

American Civil War

The American Civil War highlighted the difficulties Friends experienced in trying to reconcile their testimony against war with their staunch opposition to slavery. Many Quaker men felt duty-bound to serve in the Union army, and many Quaker women discerned a call to actively support the war effort in other ways. When the mustered-out soldiers, nurses, and others returned home after the war, most meetings quietly accepted them back without condemnation. A side effect of this action was to erode the prohibition on other forms of government service—especially political activity on behalf of the Republican Party. Voting in elections gradually became common practice again.

Political Action among Twenty-First-Century Friends

By faith we stand, and by the power of God we are upheld. Dost thou think it is by our own power and holiness we are kept from a vain conversation, from sin and wickedness?
                                                        Sarah Cheevers[19]

For the same reasons as those of eighteenth-century Friends detailed above, I stopped voting about twenty years ago. This was not a public witness; few of my friends knew. I was still a voracious consumer of news and continued to hold (and debate) political opinions. I continued to contribute to the Friends Committee on National Legislation. But in 2008, I felt compelled to vote for Barack Obama. The symbolism of an African American president was so powerful that I could not resist it. Besides, I was sure he would end the extrajudicial and immoral use of drones to assassinate those who had been declared enemies of the state. The symbolic act was successful, and I still believe it was important to elect a black man as president of the United States, but the use of organized violence in the "war on terror" increased under President Obama. For that, there is blood on my hands that I can never wash away.

Contemporary Friends are largely unaware that there was ever a time when we shunned politics, voting, and holding government office. In the United States, the prevailing view is that government action is often essential to achieve communal goals, such as justice for all people. Quakers on the whole believe that to realize our preferred outcomes we need to be active, involved citizens and voters. More than a few Friends hold office.

Governments certainly can accomplish many things, but they still reserve the right to use violence and coercion to achieve their ends. Even local governments employ armed police to protect their citizens. When an unarmed motorist is shot, all voters deserve a share of the responsibility for that death. In the face of this, Friends continue to have a fundamental obligation to model an alternative to human governance. I believe one of the greatest contemporary challenges to faithfulness for the Religious Society of Friends is this: to put our trust in God and demonstrate to others that relinquishing political activity is not shirking an essential civic responsibility but shouldering a greater burden.

Chapter 3: Changes in Quaker Faith and Practice over Time

To use words that may make many contemporary Quakers uncomfortable, this may be a way in which we need to take up our daily cross—to be patterns and examples of another way to live with each other, with the rest of creation, and with its Creator.

Quaker Testimonies

Exterior Forms are but temporary Matters. They are no Essentials of true Christianity. . . . It radically ariseth from a living, abiding, increasing Principle in Man, of a pure, spiritual and heavenly Nature. As this is cordially embraced, it enlarges in the Soul, expels the Works and Power of Darkness, and produceth its own genuine Fruits of Humility, Self-denial, Patience, Resignation to God, and Trust in him alone; Righteousness, Holiness, Meekness, Gentleness, Temperance, Goodness, Brotherly-kindness, Charity.

Joseph Phipps[20]

In court, a 'testimony' is a statement of what has been directly witnessed. A 'witness' testifies to what he or she personally saw or heard—attesting to outward, visible, or hearable things. Through the actions of the Inward Light, seventeenth-century Friends became aware of overwhelming transformations in their lives. They experienced changes in their relationships with God that prompted alterations in their outward behavior. Being drawn closer to God resulted in new and different ways of relating to each other and to the whole of creation. These Friends did not claim credit for transforming themselves or for the resulting ways in which they acted. They simply reported that they had been changed. New, outward behaviors arose as outgrowths of a profound inward conversion. New visible activities witnessed to the fact of being invisibly drawn towards the Divine. These were not things they chose to do in order to prove themselves righteous or to move themselves Godward.

Quaker testimonies are the fruits, not the roots, of a faithful relationship with God.

When understood in this sense, a Quaker testimony is an outward expression of divine love as felt in an individual's heart. The action of that love wins over the soul, altering how she or he acts, and that, in turn, can change others. This led the first Friends to violate social conventions by forswearing customary signs of respect and honor. They were not seeking attention or desiring to be rude and insulting. Being a scold has never been a Quaker testimony. They were not engaged in outward acts committed to protest an oppressive social structure. When they failed to tip their hats or used 'thou' to address social superiors, it was a loving witness directed to others' consciences—calling on them to open their inward, spiritual eyes and see what the inflowing Light of Christ revealed in their hearts. This was "answering that of God in every one"; it was a way of acknowledging God's love in each person and echoing that love in their own behavior.

In so witnessing, Friends advanced the love of enemies as integral to their testimony. This is apparent, for example, in the work of John Woolman. When he traveled in the ministry to speak about the evils of slavery, he was fervent in exposing the physical and spiritual harm done to the slave and equally distressed by the spiritual harm it evoked in the slaveholder. Woolman's opposition to slavery did not lead him to hate the one and love the other.

Personal Testimony

There is an essential difference between a personal witness and a corporate testimony. For something to be called a "Quaker testimony," it must be characteristic of the whole Society of Friends. This does not dismiss or diminish the importance of faithful action by an individual who feels compelled to behave in a way that differs from others. Individual actions may be firmly rooted in faithfulness to divine guidance and inspired by the Inward Light, and they may be the work of that person alone. This can be a trying burden, weighing on the conscience and allowing no relief for anything short of complete obedience. Even when we believe we have heard a message intended for the whole Society, we need to remember that each of us hears the still, small voice imperfectly and partially. It may be that a Friend is mistaken, but then again, we must be open to the possibility that she or he may be in advance of the rest of the community and pointing the way forward. One such example is Benjamin Lay (1681–1759), who felt called to repeatedly and dramatically denounce slavery for many years before the Society as a whole was ready to take that step. He had no choice—it was what faithfulness demanded of him. Lay was disowned by his meeting in 1738 as a result.

Individual witness is important, but in this section I address those behaviors that have been discerned as binding on the Society of Friends as a whole.

Our Corporate Testimonies

Gradually I began to understand what Friends meant by God being present in every person, not only people within the Religious Society of Friends, but people universally. I saw God in the homeless person, in the drug addict, in my brothers and sisters who differed from me in their sexual orientation, in their mental or physical capabilities, even in those whose religious views differed significantly from mine. I saw humanity as I saw myself—all of us made in the image and likeness of the Divine.

Deborah Saunders[21]

There was no list of Quaker testimonies in the seventeenth century, but over the last three hundred and fifty years numerous outward characteristics have distinguished Friends from others. William Penn's marks of a true Christian (see chapter 2) listed a few of these. Some, like wearing "plain clothes" or refusing to offer "hat honor" to social superiors, have come and gone. You might think this means those behaviors were not really Quaker testimonies—that they were missteps and were corrected in time. But outward signs of spiritual witness need to be understood in the context of a particular social milieu. The outward appearance of a testimony changes over time because it reflects the workings of the Spirit on human hearts within a particular cultural moment.

According hat honor (tipping your hat) to one's superiors was considered a normal and entirely reasonable social expectation in seventeenth-century English culture. Refusing to cooperate with that custom had a well-recognized meaning in that time and place. It was confrontational. It poked at social convention and exposed the pride of the person who awaited it. Today, people might smile if you tipped your hat to them, but almost no one would even notice if you refused to do so. Even if you pointed it out, it would probably elicit no more than a shrug. Times have changed; hat honor no longer matters.

While that particular outward act no longer has the power to testify to another person, its target, unjustified human pride, remains alive today. Since different outward behaviors feed it, different forms of witness are needed to confront it.

Chapter 3: Changes in Quaker Faith and Practice over Time

Class differences have not disappeared but are expressed in altered ways in modern cultures. For example, homeless people form an underclass today. We might think this is an issue for others to manage—the government or social service professionals. I know I would rather not have to contend with homeless people when I walk down the street or have to decide whether and how to respond to begging. But as a Quaker, I am charged with answering the Light of God shining within them, and I have to ask myself how to reflect God's love in my encounters with them. Here I have to confess that I too frequently fail.

Unlike the Children of the Light, a large part of our Society today is privileged—especially those who live in English-speaking countries. Rather than being called to challenge others' self-importance, we need to become more aware of how our own pride, implicit entitlement, and sense of superiority is spiritually wounding us. We need to witness to our own need for humility.

The Evolution of a Quaker Witness: The Testimony against War

> *We are a People that follow after those things that make for Peace, Love, and Unity, it is our desire that others feet may walk in the same, and do deny and beare our Testimony against all Strife, and Wars, and Contentions that come from the Lusts that warr in the members, that warr against the Soul, which we wait for and watch for in all People, and love and desire the good of all.*
>
> *Margaret Fell*[22]

Since all witness is directed to others at a particular time and place, its outward form naturally adapts as the years pass, but that is not the only reason for change. Some testimonies unfold over time as the members of the Society of Friends come to more fully understand what we have been called to do as a people. What is now called the peace testimony illustrates this development.

A testimony against war is one of the oldest Quaker witnesses. Like many of our earliest testimonies, it was initially a negative statement: Friends opposed war or, to be more accurate, many (but not all) early Friends refused to personally participate in war. For example, when George Fox was invited to be a captain in Oliver Cromwell's New Model Army, he refused, but not because he opposed Parliament's goals in the English Civil Wars. He said he "lived in the virtue of that life and power that took away the occasion of all wars"[23] and therefore he could not fight with "carnal weapons" for any cause.

But although Fox declared that he could not fight, he accepted that the state had the power, the right, and the God-given authority to engage in armed conflict. In 1658 Fox wrote a letter to Cromwell in which he pleads with the Lord Protector of the Commonwealth to invade (Catholic) Spain and (Muslim) Turkey and to overthrow the pope in Rome. Fox also praised the fighting prowess of Quaker soldiers and protested when the army sought to expel them.

Thus, in the first incarnation of the peace testimony, Quakers felt called to refuse individual involvement in warfare, but they recognized the necessity for others to fight. Even the 1660 declaration to King Charles—often cited as the founding statement of the Quaker peace testimony—accepts the use of "the magistrate's sword" to maintain order within the nation. In short, early Friends were not pacifists in the modern sense of the word.

An early step in the evolution of the testimony against war was evident a generation later when William Penn listed rejecting "all war among Christians" as characteristic of Friends. By the middle

Chapter 3: Changes in Quaker Faith and Practice over Time

of the next century, most Quakers had withdrawn from government service because it entangled them in the French and Indian War. At about the same time, some Friends first took a stand against paying those taxes specifically enacted to pay for war. This was not an issue on which the Society found unity then, and it remains an individual witness today.

Over the next two centuries, refusal to serve in the military or to personally participate in wars expanded into a general opposition to all war, but it was only in the twentieth century that this anti-war witness became an affirmative testimony for peace.

From the 1750s until the advent of the American Civil War, many Friends were involved in abolition work. Although this was not portrayed at the time as related to their historic opposition to war, I believe it prepared the Society to begin to see how organized state violence and systematic interpersonal violence arose from the same essential sources. Similarly, wartime (and later peacetime) relief work broadened our understanding of the nature of violence and of what is required of us. By late in the twentieth century, most Quakers had come to believe that domestic violence, racism, sexism, and poverty are all rooted in systemic violence and coercion and to feel that what is now termed the Quaker peace testimony compelled Quakers to work to ameliorate the underlying causes.

At each stage of this evolution, Friends did not consider their current position as intermediate or incomplete. It was as fully developed a witness as had been given us at that time. Only by attending to the continuing revelations of the Holy Spirit as they unfolded did we come to see the extent of the work we were divinely inspired to do. I believe our current understanding of the peace testimony is still partial and imperfect. It will continue to evolve under divine guidance.

SPICES

As individuals and as a meeting we are pulled out of our center when we let anything become that center other than God. This is one of the ways the dark forces destroy us at our core. It is a seductive energy that tells us to become involved in the lives of others, with problems and causes. All this is well and good as long as God is at the helm. However, it is easy to get ahead of God.

Louise Wilson[24]

What we commonly call testimonies today are very different from Friends' practices of three hundred and fifty years ago. For many Friends, "the Quaker testimonies" are a clearly delimited set of topics encapsulated in the mnemonic SPICES: Simplicity, Peace, Integrity, Community, Equality, and Sustainability. What they may not know is that these are of relatively recent origin, having been identified as "the testimonies" only over the last seventy years. In singling these few categories out, we have changed the character of the Quaker witness to the world.

This list gives the impression that it is a definitive inventory of official testimonies. It treats them as distinct and separate categories—each a thing in itself—and not, of necessity, part of a larger whole. One danger is that the SPICES become philosophical ideals, each to be pursued in itself. Practicing them becomes what we choose to do in order to be "good Quakers." They can develop into standards for organizing our lives that we may feel demonstrate divine favor and become sources of pride and self-righteousness. Worse, we risk implicitly turning them into idols, i.e., things we have set our hearts on, taking the place of God.

Chapter 3: Changes in Quaker Faith and Practice over Time

When we witness to our relationship with the Divine, our outward behaviors will arise from a single cause—the workings of the Inward Light acting within us—and a single response—our faithfulness in striving to bring to fruition God's longings for us. The six SPICES categories are only some of the interconnected outward behaviors that characterize a way of life. When we live faithfully—you might say, when we walk in the Light—we are Quakers all the time, no matter how embarrassing, costly, or dangerous that might be. Then we can no more choose how to testify with our lives than a truthful witness can decide what testimony to give in court. As with the Children of the Light, faithful behaviors arise as the fruits of our individual relationships with the Divine.

Traveling in the Ministry

Mary Fisher, a religious Maiden, of whose Sufferings we have before spoken in our Account of New-England, *being returned from thence to* London, *found herself concerned to go with a Message from the Lord, as she believed, to Sultan* Mahomet the Fourth, *then encamped with his Army near* Adrianople.

Joseph Besse[25]

Some of the Publishers of Truth were absolutely fearless in their determination to spread the Quaker gospel. Many Quakers today are familiar with the story of Mary Fisher, a servant who felt called to minister to the sultan of the Ottoman Turks. And there were many others who heeded a call to travel in the ministry despite the dangers. Some died. Among these was William Leddra, who went to Boston in 1661 knowing that three Friends, Marmaduke Stephenson, William Robinson, and Mary Dyer, had been executed the previous year for the crime of being publicly

Quaker in the Puritans' colony. These ministers didn't seek to be martyrs, but they didn't turn away at the prospect. They were on fire with the Spirit of God and had no choice.

In the first generation, these were explicitly missionary travels. The "Valiant Sixty" were sent out two by two, in keeping with Jesus' model of dispatching pairs of disciples in chapter 10 of Luke's gospel. These Friends went to preach again an old message to the world. They called on people to turn from Darkness to the Light of Christ.

Early on, Margaret Fell served to coordinate their travels and to direct money to them as needed. Later, the Second Morning Meeting in London was created to provide mutual support and guidance to traveling ministers. In addition to missionary work for the nascent Society of Friends, this meeting was charged with considering the needs of existing communities of worshippers. In particular, it judged which congregations were in need of a visit from an experienced minister. That charge required more and more of their attention in the years of persecution. The resulting turn from evangelizing to inward nurture foreshadowed the course of events in the eighteenth century, when most Quakers who were traveling in the ministry proceeded from meeting to meeting and spent much of their time visiting in the homes of those who were already part of the Society. By the early nineteenth century, Elias Hicks was unusual because of the relatively large amount of time he spent holding public meetings while traveling among Friends.

These intrasocietal trips were important, especially in North America where worship groups tended to be more geographically isolated. Yearly meetings regularly asked their ministers and elders to visit subordinate meetings to help rebind the connections between and among them. Although such itinerant ministers were useful in strengthening the links of far-flung Friends with the rest

Chapter 3: Changes in Quaker Faith and Practice over Time

of the Society, this source of strength also proved a danger. In the years leading up to the separations of the late 1820s, Elias Hicks may have been the person who traveled most widely among American Quaker meetings. To his allies, this presence bolstered the members of remote meetings who may have been wavering in their commitment to fundamental Quaker principles. But for those who believed him to be spreading dangerous and heretical views, his visits were broadcasting a spiritual disease. Traveling in parallel at the same time were numbers of English Friends with very different theological beliefs. They crossed the ocean intending to educate American Friends in true Quakerism. Whatever the intent of Hicks or the British travelers, rather than sustaining the Society, these visits helped stir up turmoil in the American meetings and contributed to the subsequent rifts.

In more recent times, visits among meetings have become much rarer. Perhaps as a consequence, monthly meetings have become more detached from each other. Many Friends now subscribe to a congregational model in which each church or meeting sees itself as essentially independent, although in voluntary association with others. This has had the effect of reducing quarterly and yearly meetings from decision-making to advisory bodies and as largely social and educational occasions.

As the numbers of those traveling in the ministry decreased, other forms of communication partially compensated. Orthodox, Wilburite, and Hicksite Friends each published periodicals that helped to maintain connections between widespread Friends in the nineteenth century. These were supplemented in the United States by gatherings that drew Quakers from across yearly meetings' boundaries in the second half of the century. The Friends United Meeting and Friends General Conference both grew out of such gatherings.

Educational conferences, such as the one in 1895 in Manchester, England, provided other opportunities for Friends to meet together. These led to the establishment of Quaker centers such as Woodbrooke in England; Pendle Hill, Quaker Hill, and Ben Lomond in the United States; Silver Wattle in Australia; and others. The internet offers an additional rich variety of resources.

While each of these forms of communication has been of value to some, simple meeting-to-meeting intervisitation may still be the best way to link Quakers with each other.

Chapter 4
How Primitive Quakerism Revived Would Look

> *As we have often heard said, so I believe, that ancient Quakerism is primitive Christianity revived, and as long as primitive Christianity has a practical advocate, ancient Quakerism will live and not die.*
>
> Ann Branson[1]

What would it look like if Friends revived the essential principles of seventeenth-century Quakerism? The contemporary religious environment and civil structures are quite different from those of the 1600s, but whether in the first world or the third world, these still support a social order that is in many ways diametrically opposed to the values that animated early Quakerism. Our calling as a people of God has not been fulfilled.

Three fundamental challenges remain that will shape the way a revived Society of Friends will look to the surrounding world:

- Do we put God at the center of everything we do?
- Do we model a radically faithful society that is in the world but not of the world?
- Do we form faithful communities that worship together in love, trust, patience, joy, and humility?

I believe that when we face up to these challenges, our lives and our communities will be marked by joy.

Putting God at the Center

Religion isn't something to be added to our other duties, and thus make our lives yet more complex. The life with God is the center of life, and all else is remodeled and integrated by it. It gives the singleness of eye. The most important thing is not to be perpetually passing cups of cold water to a thirsty world. We can get so fearfully busy trying to carry out the second great commandment, 'Thou shalt love they neighbor as thyself,' that we are under-developed in our devoted love to God. But we must love God as well as neighbor.

Thomas Kelly[2]

The first prerequisite for a revitalized Religious Society of Friends is putting God at the center of our lives and our spiritual communities. To do that, we need to invite the Inward Light to search our hearts and illuminate our souls. Like the early Quakers, we need to stand still in the Spiritual Light so that we can see the Spiritual Darkness we harbor and identify what we have placed at the center of our lives. The Inward Light exposes our Inward Darkness and allows us to know and to feel how evil has captured our spirits. When that happens, our first response may be that it is impossible to be free of that Darkness.

Many Friends, I believe, are centered on doing good—and Friends are good at doing. Our consciences are pricked by one good cause and then another and another until nothing remains for God. As Thomas Kelly also wrote, "Too many of us have too many irons in the fire. We get distracted by the intellectual claim to our interest in a thousand and one good things, and before we

Chapter 4: How Primitive Quakerism Revived Would Look

know it we are pulled and hauled breathlessly along by an overburdened program of good committees and good undertakings."[3]

As a whole, members of the Religious Society of Friends have accomplished far more than our numbers would seem to justify, but busyness isn't a calling, neither for an individual nor a community. When we put it at the center of our lives, it can take up every minute of our time and every ounce of our energy. Worse, our lack of free time can become an excuse for avoiding taking on those things that we have been uniquely called to do. We can easily become too diligent and conscientious to have room for God. When we let the good things we do engulf us, they become idols—objects of our devotion that take the place of God in our hearts. Even undeniably good works can become idols if they are not the tasks we have been divinely called to do. Early Friends called this will-worship—putting our own will ahead of God's will. Today, we might call it exercising our freedom to choose for ourselves, but it is still putting our own judgments first.

If we are self-aware and honest, some of us will realize we have put ourselves at the center of our being. The culture of Western civilization teaches us from birth that we can and should be the masters of our destiny—that we have an absolute right to choose what we will do with our lives. We are told to follow our dreams and to do what our hearts desire. Free will is, of course, a divine gift, but when we choose to put our desires ahead of what God hopes for us, we raise our aspirations up as our highest values. They become our idols, and we become the objects of our worship.

The Spirit of the World tempts us with money and worldly comfort, power and public acclaim. Advertising bombards us with promises of happiness derived from the things we buy or see or do. It leads us to believe we don't have time for religion. Oh, maybe we will later, but not now. But when we trust Providence to guide us, we will find we have all the time and energy we need.

Being in the World but Not of the World

Christ designed that His followers should be in the world, but not of the world. The churches were planted in the cities; now we find in many places our meetinghouses are built in some quiet, retired, out of the way spot, as far as may be from the wicked world, instead of standing as a light in the world.
Elizabeth Comstock[4]

From its beginning, the Society of Friends saw itself as a chosen people. They had been called to be a light unto the nations. Their relationships with each other and with God modeled an intentional way of living very different from that of the people who lived around them. Especially in the decades immediately following the royal restoration in 1660, they believed they were living in a land dominated by the wicked spirit of this world. The outward life promoted by that spirit was centered on accumulating earthly wealth and power and on demanding undeserved respect and recognition, false glory, and hollow honors. Many of the most prominent people squandered their lives on vain amusements and profligate entertainments. God and religion were peripheral to the leaders of Restoration England. They were useful to the powerful only to the extent that they buttressed a social system that upheld their place in society.

The primary ways in which we interact with the outside world today are economic. Financial fears and insecurity dominate the lives of many people. A good job with benefits and a solid retirement plan are held to be essential for a happy life. Earning money, holding money, saving money, and especially spending

Chapter 4: How Primitive Quakerism Revived Would Look

money are judged to be the most important endeavors of a successful life. Fear of being penniless shadows us at every stage of our lives. For example, these have been just some of my fears: Will I have enough to feed my children and afford a safe place to live? Can I afford to pay for the education and training I need to find better employment? Will I be able to retire? Will I outlive my resources or run out of money when I am old and helpless?

Reviving primitive Quakerism is simply seeing Penn's "Main Fundamental in Religion" act in us and freely allowing it to guide our lives. This isn't private or personal. It isn't a set of purely spiritual practices that can be practiced out of the sight of others. It happens in the full sight of the whole world. When a person yields to the guidance of the Light Within, that self-surrender naturally and inevitably becomes visible in her or his everyday life.

This is what it means to be in the world but not of the world. It means we are Friends all the time, that we live up to that standard in every outward action and with every spoken word. It means our communities visibly witness to the world.

Community

Our life is love, and peace, and tenderness; and bearing one with another, and forgiving one another, and not laying accusations one against another; but praying one for another, and helping one another up with a tender hand.

Isaac Penington[5]

The word "community" is used a lot in contemporary Western culture. It is used as a way to sort and identify the people we encounter and to delineate our relationships with them. We tend to think of communities as being demarked in one of two ways. There are those in which you are involuntarily enrolled by birth or by a physical characteristic, such as the Greek community or the deaf community. And then there are the communities you voluntarily choose to be in, such as the bicycling community or the Rotary Club.

The importance of communities in Western culture is highlighted by the roles they play in some of the West's most divisive issues. For example, affirmative action policies are based on the premise that members of some communities have suffered past discrimination and are therefore entitled to compensatory action now. How we distinguish between these two types of communities—for example, whether we believe a woman to be a lesbian by choice or by birth—has implications for how we are morally obligated to treat members of particular communities.

Although this dichotomy is useful in many situations and may seem to be all-encompassing, it neglects a third type of community, the kind the Friends of Truth felt they were in. They believed that the Society of Friends was a community of people who had heard a divine call to come together and who had responded to that call. In doing so, they became a covenant community—they were bound to the Infinite Spirit and, through that binding, to each other. The earliest Quakers became members of the Society of Friends because the Inward Light shepherded them to it.

Community as Testimony

We encounter each other as a people of faith with faith in ourselves and faith in each other. . . . We have been growing and we need to look forward to growing further in our understanding of ourselves as a people who have a task, to make this a better world as we continue to minister.

Gladys Kang'ahi[6]

Chapter 4: How Primitive Quakerism Revived Would Look

My yearly meeting is revising its *Book of Faith and Practice*, and I serve on the committee charged with producing drafts for consideration. The testimonies often referred to by the acronym SPICES were not included when the current version was written in 1978, but the committee decided these testimonies have come to play a prominent a role in the spiritual lives of Friends in the yearly meeting and thus need to be addressed in the new edition. We were making good progress until we came to the subsection on community. One committee member asked, "How is community a testimony?"

The questioner was an experienced and weighty Friend, and the question was genuine. In her experience, 'community' was something Friends created with and for each other. It was not a witness to the wider world. These communities are inwardly directed places in which Quakers meet together, encounter one another, and provide support for each other. But if something is a testimony, it is focused externally—it testifies to others.

If we are divinely called to model an alternative society, one that is characterized by a unique relationship with our Creator and the whole of creation, we can't do it surreptitiously. We can't hide our light under a bushel; in a revived Society, our communities are manifest public witnesses.

Outreach

No single person can build the foundation of a healthy Quaker church or meeting—it requires a community of faithful Friends. In the Western world, we have seen a transformation in the understanding of what constitutes a religious community over the last four hundred years. In the seventeenth century, it was assumed that a congregation was assembled by God. Men and women were called into a particular community and faithfully responded to that calling. They assumed that the Comforter cares about us individually, has a purpose for each of us, and is active in the world.

In a perverse way, being reviled and persecuted, sometimes harshly, validated the worshippers who were thus assembled. Unless they truly believed the Holy Spirit was leading them to do so, why would anyone choose to associate with those wretched Quakers?

Many now see their religious affiliation as self-determined and their congregation as self-assembled. They believe their congregation was brought together purely as the by-product of personal preferences and individual choices. It is assumed that individuals choose a particular religious body because it appeals to them and because they believe it will meet their needs. New members decide to join, but it is assumed that their commitment is conditional, not covenantal. If another option feels better, they will leave.

If we start with these assumptions, we will see outreach as a process designed to recruit new members. By implication, membership is viewed as a commodity to be advertised and sold in the religious marketplace. That in turn leads to particular questions that frame outreach activities: How can we make ourselves uniquely attractive? How do we make it easy to join? What benefits do we offer that others do not?

When you put up your house for sale, you clean up the yard, update the kitchen, and apply a fresh coat of paint to make it look more attractive. Do we try to 'sell' Quakerism the same way? Do we make it as undemanding as possible so it's easy for others to feel comfortable among us?

'Convinced' has become one of the treasured words in the Quaker dialect. The goal of an outreach program is often to

Chapter 4: How Primitive Quakerism Revived Would Look

convince as many people as possible, but the way such a campaign is conducted may be based on a misunderstanding of what that word meant in the seventeenth century. Back then, if someone was convinced in court, they were found guilty; that is, they were convicted. In the same way, new Friends in those days would say they were convinced because the Light Within had shown them their spiritual guilt—they had been convinced or convicted of their sins. When we speak of people being convinced today, we usually mean they have engaged in an intellectual exercise that resulted in a decision based on facts and logic. If we are looking to convince new members, we may think we need to attract them by appealing to their minds.

If we believe that new recruits will weigh the costs and benefits of Quakerism and decide whether our case is logically compelling, we will be led to recruit by persuasion. Then, finding new members becomes a program of activities we plan and carry out in order to change their minds. When, as so often happens, this fails to accomplish its goal, we feel we just haven't found the right arguments to persuade them.

But what if the primitive Quakers were right? The Society of Friends grew by leaps and bounds during the 1650s and continued to gain in numbers in the following years when Quakers were being persecuted. Although some of this growth resulted from the evangelism of traveling ministers, Friends' principle "outreach" activity was to regularly meet for worship. They ignored the English statute that required all religious services to use the Anglican *Book of Common Prayer*. Unlike many other persecuted sects, Friends refused to go into hiding. They held their meetings for worship at their regular times and in their regular, public places. That made it easy for the authorities to harass and arrest them.

One of those ready targets was the Reading (England) Meeting. On Sunday, May 1, 1664, the local justice showed up during meeting for worship. This was not the first time he had come to disrupt worship, so it was no surprise to those present when he declared the meeting to be an illegal assembly and arrested all the adult men who were present. The next Sunday, he returned. Since there were no men in attendance, he arrested the adult women. Two weeks later, he reappeared to find only children and "young maidens" quietly assembled. He tried to drive them off, brutally striking one with his staff and threatening to arrest them as well, but the children stayed in their places. He continued to harass Reading Friends for at least the next eight years, at one point chopping up all the seats and nailing the door to the meetinghouse shut, but meetings for worship persisted. As William Penn wrote, "It was not very easie to our *Primitive Friends* to make themselves *Sights* and *Spectacles*, and the Scorn and Derision of the World."[7]

Not very easy, but they did it.

The men, women, and children in Reading Meeting believed that the Inward Teacher had called them to that meeting and that they could not be anywhere else on a Sunday morning. Their personal comfort didn't matter. Loss of freedom didn't change their minds. Today we do not live under state-sanctioned persecution. Perhaps if we did, we too would find that kind of courage. Even so, we can ask what lessons this story has for our outreach activities. Here are a few suggestions:

- Be present. Treat attending meeting for worship as the most important thing you can do on Sunday.
- Be visible. Meet in a place where you can be easily found and publicly announce the time and place of your meeting for worship.

- Trust God. The Inward Light will guide people to you.
- Feed the people who attend meeting for worship spiritually. People won't come back because you serve cookies; they will if you feed their souls.

Mutual Accountability and Love

The mutual Love, subsisting between the faithful Followers of Christ, is more pure than that Friendship which is not seasoned with Humility, how specious soever the Appearance.
John Woolman[8]

One big difference between a Quaker community in the United States today and one in earlier times is the degree to which the prior one was willing to involve itself in the lives of its members. For most of our history, Friends saw themselves as being in a covenant community—a group gathered to be a people of God. Being part of a covenant community entailed mutual spiritual and temporal obligations of each other, to each other, and for each other. They willingly submitted to the authority of the meeting and accepted the meeting's discernment on important issues.

Today, we remember John Woolman as a spiritual giant, but in his day, when he felt called to travel in the ministry and preach against slavery, he first asked permission from his home meeting before making any plans. Usually the meeting said yes, but sometimes it said no. "No" didn't mean the meeting had decided that he was wrong in his opposition to slavery or that he should give up his travels in the ministry, only that they had discerned that the path he was proposing was not the right one at that time. Woolman didn't attempt to win them over with carefully crafted arguments and compelling, persuasive words. He entrusted the work of changing hearts to the Holy Spirit and accepted that his personal sense of what he should be doing could be wrong. And so, he waited for his meeting's endorsement before proceeding.

This kind of submission to the discernment of the community is much less common today. A major reason for this is the way in which Western culture has changed. Individualism is now celebrated in a way that it was not before. Personal freedom, individual rights, and privacy are held up as supreme values in ways they were not previously. Many today believe that each of us is responsible to God alone and that our meeting's proper role is to be a source of support and comfort. The idea that it is a place of counsel and guidance—that we should submit a leading to the authority of the meeting and trust its discernment over our own—is un-American.

On the surface, according such authority to the meeting echoes the paternalism, patriarchy, and racism that were prevalent in our past and, we must admit, still live in the secret places of our hearts. In the face of these concerns, a revived Quakerism depends on mutual trust and on members having the humility to submit to each other—not some submitting to others but each to each and all to all. This is one of the most important ways our communities can testify to the world. By building loving covenant communities, we model countercultural ways of relating to each other—ways that are mutually accountable, trusting, and loving.

How, you may ask, do we achieve this? It is not something that can be done by decree or a collective act of will. Trust is gained bit by bit. It grows out of love, humility, and risk. Ultimately, we can only learn to trust the discernment of the community by experience.

Chapter 4: How Primitive Quakerism Revived Would Look

Membership

The Origins of Membership

Our Society originated, grew stronger, and flourished under persecution, and the members were united in the strong bonds of mutual love and affection, which qualified them to deeply feel for each other, and made them willing to share in each other's sufferings.

Sunderland Gardner[9]

Some Quakers today have the misconception that for its first seventy years, there was no membership in the Religious Society of Friends and, when membership arose, it was a purely administrative action of no great significance. It is true that the first formal lists of members were compiled in the 1720s, but the recording of those lists did not mark a change in early Friends' understanding of what it meant to be part of the Society. Quakers considered themselves members of a unique Society from its earliest days.

The English Parliament was not confused about who was or was not a Friend when it enacted the Quaker Act of 1662, which forbade five or more members of the Society from meeting together in worship. When the Society was being persecuted, it wasn't necessary to record membership, nor was it necessary to check official records to see who was a Quaker; all that was needed was to wait and see who showed up on Sunday morning. Who risked incarceration? Those who freely and publicly associated with that reviled minority were by definition members, while any who claimed to be members but hid themselves away were not.

This definition allowed a wide degree of latitude for beliefs, but that doesn't mean the early Quakers' sense of membership was vague or equivocal. Even in those early years, they disowned those whom they discerned to be out of harmony with the community; a person cannot be stripped of his or her membership unless it is something already possessed. When, as William Penn noted, some were found to be "Refractory to this Good and Wholesom Order settled among them,"[10] they would first be admonished and labored with, and if they continued to resist it would be declared publicly that they were not members of the Society. The willingness to disown delineated the boundaries of the community. Membership is as old as Quakerism.

Membership in the Twenty-First Century

Things have changed over the years. When the church or meeting is viewed as a voluntary association of independent individuals, that changes the meaning of membership and makes the congregation fragile. That can undermine its willingness to challenge behaviors that are inconsistent with good order.

In recent years, cases of inappropriate behavior—especially those involving the abuse of children—have led to disownment, but we really prefer to avoid conflict. Divergent beliefs may be consciously ignored. In some cases, we make those who are "not like us" uncomfortable and silently rejoice if they decide to move on to another spiritual home. Even this is rare because so many of our meetings and churches are small and may fear that the loss of even a single individual could threaten its continued existence. Failure to act in a timely manner can reinforce the sense that it is just a voluntary collection of people who sit together on Sunday mornings. Such a congregation does not value membership. It is not a covenant community. It does not witness to the world as a community.

Chapter 4: How Primitive Quakerism Revived Would Look

Some contemporary Quakers object to formal membership, and they pose several good questions: Why does it matter? Can't we return to that [thought to be primordial] state in which everyone who shows up on Sunday morning is equally a part of the community? Isn't making any distinctions between people a violation of the testimony of equality?

The answer to the first question is that it matters because Quakerism does have some fundamental beliefs—they might be called Quaker doctrines. The most central of these is belief in the reality of and the transformative actions of the Light Within. The Light is a theological concept that has distinguished us from others for more than three hundred and fifty years. Anyone who rejects this basic concept is undeniably declaring that he or she is not a Friend.

Second, if any collection of people who happen to assemble on a Sunday constitutes the Society of Friends, then that name has no intrinsic meaning. It is only a transient flavor of the week.

This is not to say that there is a secret list of beliefs that all must subscribe to—that would be a creed—but a church or meeting can and should discern whether those who wish to be members share its essential beliefs. In keeping with Quaker tradition, this determination is not the rigid application of a predetermined rule but a process conducted by the local congregation. Discernment with a committee for membership furnishes applicants with an opportunity to delve deeply into their personal beliefs in a supportive and inquiring environment. In much the same way, each time a church or meeting undertakes to discern whether an applicant should be taken into membership, it provides an opportunity for them to reexamine what is essential to membership in that particular faith community and what is not.

If done conscientiously, this process makes distinctions between people, but these distinctions do not serve to raise some up and diminish others. It recognizes that the Religious Society of Friends is a people called by God to do its part in the ongoing work of building the blessed community on earth. We have our own peculiar spiritual path. It is a course mapped out for us by the Holy Spirit, and it is not the right path for everyone.

I have five brothers. One has remained Roman Catholic his whole life. Two years in Nepal and marriage to a woman from a very different religious background only served to confirm his Catholicism. Another brother attended a Quaker meeting for a while and then returned to the Catholic Church. A third brother converted to Islam, and the other two are each very active in two (very different) Protestant churches. We all take our spiritual lives seriously—none is in a religious community out of convenience or inertia. Each of us has searched for the path that God has chosen for him. We are each distinct. We each have different callings, and, I believe, each has found his right path. It would be spiritual hubris for me to believe that my path would be better for my brothers. It would be wrong for one of my brothers to be taken into membership with Friends.

Meeting for Worship

The Lord of Heaven and Earth we found to be near at hand; and as we waited upon him in pure Silence, our Minds out of all things, his Dreadful Power, and Glorious Majesty, and Heavenly Presence appear'd in our Assemblies, when there was no Language, Tongue nor Speech from any Creature, and the Kingdom of Heaven did gather us and catch us all, as in a Net; and his Heavenly Power at one time drew many Hundreds to Land, that we came to know a place to stand in,

Chapter 4: How Primitive Quakerism Revived Would Look

and what to wait in; and the Lord appeared daily to us, to our Astonishment, Amazement and great Admiration.

Francis Howgill[11]

The Friends of Truth spent many hours together each week in meetings for worship, but they were clear that it was not the outward practice but the inward state that mattered. They had stripped away all the externals that others considered essential to worship—hymns, scripture readings, sermons, and celebrants. What remained was the simple knowledge that God was present and reaching out to them. Being in the divine presence filled and sustained them in those hours assembled together.

They were seeking to know God, not to know *about* God.

A Worshipping Community

For Friends, worship unwraps an opportunity to enter into spiritual communion with the Word in Our Hearts and with other worshippers. It creates a sacred space in which we can be emptied of our separateness and gathered into the divine presence. This is an experience we may occasionally stumble into on our own, and not only at 10 a.m. on a Sunday morning. We may enter this divine union at any time—sometimes unexpected and unbidden—but being in the company of a community of fellow worshippers deepens, facilitates, and magnifies the experience. Each worshipper draws others along in the same way that individual droplets of water pull each other along in a stream, all flowing in the same direction.

Anything the community or an individual worshipper does to strengthen their spiritual bonds with each other helps draw the congregation in its flow Godward. The outward forms are not important, but anything that separates and leads people off in their own directions harms the worship. In some meetings, music and singing facilitates worship. Listening or joining together in song empties people of their distractions and draws them along to the deep pool of communion. In other meetings, a prepared sermon can melt the divisions among the members. But if instead the sermon gives people something to think about—conducting each into his or her own intellect and out of spiritual communion with others—it can be destructive. Divine Truth is ready to lead each of us, singly and together, if we open ourselves to its guidance.

Preparation for Worship

The Children of the Light came together prepared for worship. These were not people who spent a lot of time reading books. Books were expensive and book ownership was rare, but if a person owned a book, it was very likely a Bible. Not all were literate, but those who were literate read the Bible. Opportunities to read were limited. Daylight was precious in a society in which most labored long hours, and candles were expensive. What they had in abundance was time for reflection and time to talk with each other about those things that were important. In that society, finding inner peace with God was important. As a result, they came to meeting for worship with hours of preparation.

Worship was not time spent in solitary silence. Waiting worship was filled with the company of their fellow worshippers. They observed how others shifted in their seats, how they sighed, how they breathed. They knew when someone was weeping. They experienced the difference between a living silence and a dead silence. They listened to others speak out of the stillness. Some of the ministry they heard was good; some was not. But more than all that, they felt what it was like to be drawn into communion with the Oneness and, through that divine connection, into spiritual

Chapter 4: How Primitive Quakerism Revived Would Look

union with each other. They felt themselves being gathered together and came to recognize the signs of communion. They learned by sweet experience how it felt to center into worship.

Today, we have much more free time and many more sources of information to learn from but also many more distractions, diversions, and opportunities for entertainment. Time for quiet reflection and meditation has been squeezed out of our lives, and opportunities for conversation about things that are eternal are all too rare. Even on Sunday morning, the car ride on our way to worship is often dominated by the radio.

Practice

One first-day, being at meeting, a young woman, named Anne Wilson, was there and preached; she was very zealous, and fixing my eye upon her, she with a great zeal pointed her finger at me, uttering these words with much power, 'A traditional Quaker, thou comest to meeting as thou went from it (the last time) and goes from it as thou came to it, but art no better for thy coming, what wilt thou do in the end?' This was so pat to [in harmony with] my then condition, that, like Saul, I was smitten to the ground, as it might be said, but turning my thoughts inward, in secret I cried, Lord, what shall I do to help it? *And a voice as it were spoke in my heart saying,* Look unto me, and I will help thee; *and I found much comfort, that made me shed abundance of tears.*

Samuel Bownas[12]

When I was young, I played the piano. I had some innate ability and could pick out a tune by ear pretty well. My mother arranged lessons for me and I went with high hopes, but I didn't practice in between lessons and I never got very good. My teacher gave me assignments and I would look at them, but then I spent my time at home noodling around on the keyboard, trying to play Beatles tunes and crashing my way through favorite songs. I hated finger exercises and never learned to sight-read music. The only time I played in even a semi-disciplined way was during my lessons, and my teacher knew it. He didn't want to invest a lot effort in me. My lessons soon ended.

As I wrote that paragraph, I came to have a new appreciation for the story Samuel Bownas told. Just as he was unchanged from week to week and from meeting to meeting, I was unchanged between my piano lessons. I thought the instruction I received from the teacher would be sufficient to transform me—that I could be a passive recipient of knowledge and it would make me a better piano player. I thought if I took enough classes, I would get to be really good at playing the piano.

Sitting in expectant waiting is a skill, and, like any other skill, it can be improved with practice. Bownas hadn't practiced between meetings for worship, and neither do many Friends today, but we still expect to get good at it.

At least I listened to my teacher during the lessons instead of showing off my attempts at Beatles songs for him. And I knew I had much to learn from him. Sunday morning worship is the equivalent of a weekly lesson, with the Holy Spirit as our teacher. When we bring our own plans into our time in worship—carrying in a book to read or a journal to write in or deciding in advance a particular style of worship—we are ignoring our Teacher during our lessons. Worship is not a skill we can develop by reading about it or thinking about it; we need to do it together and under the guidance of our Teacher to get good at it. To recoup the experience that primitive Quakers experienced, we need to make time in our admittedly busy lives to sit together and to help each other learn

Chapter 4: How Primitive Quakerism Revived Would Look

how to do it well—to try and fail, to try and fail, and to try and improve.

That doesn't mean we should be lecturing others. We can best serve to bind the meeting for worship together by being an example, not a scold. Come early and help to spiritually prepare the space with your centered presence. Offer to host a midweek meeting for worship and then come whether anyone else shows up or not. Silently greet each person with love as they enter the room.

There are a lot of things we can do to build and strengthen our community. Talking with other Friends is good. Eating meals together is good. Bible study and small group discussions are good. They each can help build stronger and closer interpersonal relationships; they can enhance the social cohesion within our communities. But worship together is essential if we are to build a covenant community—a beloved community of God.

Prayer

"Thank you for everything; I have no complaints." Try saying that every day and see what happens.
                                    Peggy Senger Morrison[13]

It's hard to build and maintain a relationship without being in conversation with one another. Traditional Quaker worship is rooted in calming, quieting, and readying ourselves to hear the still small voice in our hearts and souls. Listening in the stillness is a primary way in which Friends seek to learn what God hopes for them and desires from them, but in addition to listening, it also opens a space in which we can speak in turn. It gives us a chance to thank God for all we have received, to tell God how we are doing—both the good and the bad—and to ask for the help we need. When we hold up our side of the conversation, it is an opportunity to reveal ourselves as if there were no other way for God to know us. Commonly, this is called praying.

When we pray, we expose ourselves in a profound way. We invite the Inward Guide to show us a path forward and to help us walk it. We make ourselves vulnerable to spiritual transformation.

The word 'prayer' is hard for some Quakers to use for a variety of reasons. For some, it is one of those words poisoned by bad experiences earlier in our lives, but we should not surrender the word to those who have misused it. Others may feel God is uninvolved in this world or too distant or too busy—not interested in our little lives. Or, we may have come to look on prayer as little more than a poor attempt at a magic incantation—an effort to change or control God to make God do what we want and what we think is most important. It's easy to fall into that belief when we are young, to feel disappointed when it doesn't work, and to decide praying is a waste of time. That's what happened to me, and it took a long time before I was ready to try again.

When I did, I found that all I could say amounted to variations on four prayers: "I'm sorry," "Thanks," "Help [me or others]," and "What next?"

I know God already knows the contents of my heart—my hopes and dreams, joys and fears, sorrows and regrets. I don't pray because I am afraid that God won't think to heal someone's cancer unless I bring it up. My experience is that praying doesn't change God, but the act of praying changes me. It reminds me that I am in a loving relationship with a supernatural being who is beyond my comprehension. Praying tenders my heart and humbles my mind.

Chapter 4: How Primitive Quakerism Revived Would Look

Joy

Such a discovery of an Eternal Life and Love breaking in, nay, always there, but we were too preoccupied to notice it, makes life glorious and new. And one sings inexpressibly sweet songs within oneself, and one tries to keep one's inner hilarity and exuberance within bounds . . . I'd rather be jolly Saint Francis hymning his canticle to the sun than a dour old sobersides Quaker whose diet would appear to have been spiritual persimmons.

Thomas Kelly[14]

Joy, like faith, is not something we can order up on demand or decide we will possess. Despite what our consumerist culture promises, joy cannot be purchased. It is a gift. Like love, it is something we can invite and something we can make ourselves vulnerable to. We open ourselves to joy by creating the conditions in which joy flourishes. I believe living in concert with the guidance of the Inward Light removes impediments to joy.

Why So Glum?

It's easy to slip into being "a dour old sobersides Quaker," and that's a stumbling block in the path to joy—both for ourselves and for those we might hope would come join us. This has certainly been part of our reputation for many years, for understandable reasons. Many early Friends believed they were living in the end times—that the world as they knew it was coming to its culmination. That is a sobering thought, one that would naturally lead to a strict and vigilant way of living. Likewise, in order to survive decades of persecution, Friends sought to be blameless— evident righteousness was an explicit defense against all unfair accusations.

127

Even after the passage of the Act of Toleration, Quakers remained a despised minority and had to endure the weight of "the World's" judgment. This was undoubtedly one of the factors that pressed the Society to adopt strict outward patterns of behavior such as wearing the plain clothes and speaking the plain speech and to enforce them with the threat of disownment. It is no surprise that, as mentioned above, William Penn listed "against worldly sports and pastimes" and "against the observance of so-called holy days, public fasts, or feasts" as two of the marks of a true Christian.

However, some of the foremost first Friends resisted such a colorless and joyless existence. In her last pastoral letter to Friends, Margaret Fell Fox (without success) wrote:

> Wee must looke at no Collours, nor make anything that is changeable Collours as the hilles are, nor sell them, nor wear them. But wee must bee all in one Dress, and one collour. This is a silly poor Gospel.[15]

As a side effect, putting such outward requirements into practice induced the Society to withdraw from engagement with others, hopelessly seeking earthly purity by hedging itself off from "the World."

On an individual level, internalizing such constraints could lead to constantly guessing (and second-guessing) what God required of one, fostering a gloomy and duty-bound existence. Outward behavior smothered inward joy. Inevitably, for some it also degenerated from seeking righteousness to being self-righteous.

Our rightly celebrated history of social action may have further contributed to a dour disposition. Progress is slow and achievements are limited, making the work discouraging. For example, being the first religious body to reject slavery in the British Empire meant that Friends waited many long, disheartening years before they saw the realization of legal abolition. Related to

Chapter 4: How Primitive Quakerism Revived Would Look

this, Friends' centuries of opposition to war did not bring about universal peace; in fact, it was the breathtakingly vast violence of the Civil War that brought about the emancipation of slaves in the United States. Moreover, in the century and a half since then, Friends have been aware of how much more is needed to achieve true racial equality, how slowly progress has come, and how often a step forward has been followed by two steps back. This can be emotionally and spiritually debilitating.

Rejoicing over small victories can highlight the enormous challenges that remain.

Love

I am not writing to discourage you with memories of past tests and trials or with reminders of the immensity of the unfinished tasks. I don't believe that God wants us be "dour old sobersides." Nor do I believe that putting God at the center of our lives and our religious communities is a prescription for "spiritual persimmons."

What marked the work of many of our spiritual ancestors was not grim determination so much as a deep-seated belief in the transformational power of God's love to change the world and in our ability to transmit that love. Take, for example, Lucretia Mott, who dedicated her life to seeking an end to war, the abolition of slavery, and the recognition of the rights of women. Her stated instrument was "the faith that works by love, and purifies the heart."[16] Hers was often lonely work and the victories were manifestly partial, but she wrote, "True religion makes not men gloomy. . . . We know well that there are sacrifices to make in our life, in the pursuit of our duty, the attempt to uplift the lowly . . . but always we feel the conviction that we enter into life thereby and its rich experiences."[17] Lucretia Mott was preserved and upheld by the joy that comes from doing the work to which she felt God called her.

This is not just a Quaker idea. Pope Francis is a living example of how to live a God-centered life. He is a deeply religious and profoundly spiritual man. Francis is obviously motivated by an enlightened social conscience (or, as Friends might say, he faithfully follows the guidance of the Inward Light of Christ) and is visibly filled to overflowing with joy. Francis lives and acts as if he can depend on God—and so can we.

Quaker Optimism

Why, the millennium is here; the kingdom of God has come. This is what we should preach. Oh, that the fruits of this divine spirit should appear, which are love, peace, joy, goodness, truth! the spirit that is first gentle, pure, full of mercy, full of good fruits. Here is no disparagement of good works.

Lucretia Mott[18]

Our Society is no longer persecuted or reviled—in fact, we are widely admired. The self-imposed outward impediments to happiness are long gone. For better or worse, we don't feel constrained from engaging in worldly pastimes or celebrating feasts and holidays. We are free to wear "changeable Collours" and to use the same pronouns as anyone else. The hedge against the world was cut down and plowed under generations ago.

We know we are not predestined in how we act in this world. Everything may be "in God's hands," but we know our hands can make a difference. The resulting improvements may be achingly slow, but we can look back at past achievements and have a sure

Chapter 4: How Primitive Quakerism Revived Would Look

faith that the future will yield still more. Our work has not been in vain: "the millennium is here; the kingdom of God has come"!

But more than any outward changes, if we truly believe what we say about being Quakers, joy will be a natural result. We say that each person has access to the Infallible Guide (although our ability to clearly discern it may be faint and our willingness to follow it too often constrained). We know the all-loving deity by direct experience—we know we can trust in Divine Providence. There have been setbacks, but when we step back and look, we can see the kingdom of heaven being built brick by brick.

Two Essential Elements of the Quaker Way

PEACE is sown for the Righteous, and Joy and Gladness for the Upright in Heart; they are certainly Blessed and truly Happy who answer the holy Call of God by pure Obedience, as this our beloved Sister [Sarah Beck] hath done; for she chose the Truth to be her Path, and her Delight was in it even from a Child.

Robert Barrawe[19]

I have come to believe that there are two essentials to the Quaker way. On a personal level, we each enjoy the immediate guidance of the Inward Light. An individual who faithfully follows its direction will be "a good person." It doesn't matter whether you identify the Light as emanating from Christ or whether you believe in God. Following the guidance of the Inward Light will lead to a spiritually fulfilling life on earth.

Whatever may happen after death—and whether or not you believe in an afterlife—doesn't matter. If you invite the Light Within to open your mind, tender your heart, and illuminate your soul, it will shepherd you through a life that is worthy of it.

Attending to the Light will make you vulnerable to God's transforming joy.

The second essential element is a corporate one: the Society of Friends exists to model an alternative way of living on earth. My word for this way of living is "God-centered," but this invitation and challenge is open to those who do not wish to use that term. We are called to create communities that demonstrate how to love one another, how to love those who are different from us, and how to love all of creation. We are called to openly express the love that drives out fear and to foster it in others. Living this way cracks open the possibility of joy in the world.

Chapter 5
Being Leaven

In one sense, all movements of renewal are a return to an earlier vitality. Institutions can never be revived, but people can, and are.

John Punshon[1]

The apostle Paul said, "A little leaven leavens the whole loaf" (Galatians 5:9). I like to bake, and when I make a loaf of bread, I use half a teaspoon of yeast to leaven it—so little yeast that it's easily overlooked among all the ingredients laid out on the kitchen counter. I don't notice any effect when it is first mixed in, not until the dough has been allowed to sit quietly for a while. Even then, outwardly it still looks like dough, but the lump has been inwardly transformed. Each yeast cell works on the sugars and starches it is in contact with, digesting glucose and exhaling little bubbles of carbon dioxide. Each one is tiny, but together even a little bit can transform a dense glutinous mass into a spongy, leavened loaf.

A lot of Friends today are concerned about our small numbers; some worry that if we don't grow, the Society of Friends will disappear. They turn to various forms of outreach to bring more bodies into the Society. But reviving Quakerism just to prolong the existence of the Religious Society of Friends is not worth the trouble. I believe we are a chosen people—we were called into being to fulfill a divine purpose, just as God has called other peoples for other purposes. In order to fulfill our mission as a people, we need to act as leaven in this world—to help fill creation with the breath of the Holy Spirit the way bread is filled with the breath of yeast.

Accomplishing our mission requires humility. We have to remember that the loaf doesn't become yeast; the yeast becomes part of the loaf. Contrary to what some Friends hoped in the 1650s, I don't believe the whole world will ever be converted to Quakerism. We are a small people, and our numbers will probably remain small. This can become an excuse not to act until we are more numerous—believing that first we must engage in outreach—but the growth we should be seeking is a side effect of faithful action, not a prerequisite for it. Our faithfulness will preach more powerfully than anything else we might do. We need to trust that our numbers will be sufficient to accomplish the task to which we have been called and to trust that the Religious Society of Friends will endure so long as we faithfully serve the Caller.

Being leaven isn't easy. It is slow and often lonely work, but that is the nature of the leavening. A loaf of bread won't rise unless the yeast is thoroughly mixed into the much greater mass of flour, water, and other ingredients and is interspersed so thoroughly that it is no longer visible. No single yeast cell does the job alone; each one transforms the dough with which it is immediately in contact. Meanwhile, the baker waits patiently, trusting the leaven to do its work.

The Religious Society of Friends won't be revived on *our* schedule but in *God's* time. We aren't the bakers, just ingredients in a divine recipe. Yeast uses enzymes to break down and convert the starches and sugars it encounters, but the instrument we have been given is love. We may never know the effects of our presence, but

Chapter 5: Being Leaven

the love and commitment of each individual who embraces the Quaker way points others to the Inward Light for guidance and spiritual strength. The contributions of each one of us who is called are vitally important in transforming and reviving the Religious Society of Friends.

Twelve Simple Queries

From our earliest days, Friends have used queries to periodically examine their lives as individuals. In the same way, reflection on corporate queries has helped to enrich the lives of our spiritual communities. The queries below are starting points for both kinds of contemplation. Open yourself to the guidance of the Inward Light as you consider each one and see what other questions arise within you.

1. Am I a Quaker? What does that mean to me?
   What marks my spiritual community as Quaker?

2. Where is God in my life? How do I worship God?
   How is God manifest in the heart of my community?

3. What spiritual disciplines enliven my spirit and guide my days?
   How does my community facilitate spiritual growth?

4. Is my life rooted in integrity?
   How does my community help me to be truthful in all ways?

5. Who am I responsible for? Who am I responsible to?
   How does my community call me to account?

6. What binds me to my meeting community?
   What fosters mutual love and spiritual communion among us?

7. When have I been led to seek the will of God?
   Does my community engage in spiritual discernment?

8. How do I avoid temporal and spiritual distractions?
   Is my community willing to let go of unnecessary practices?

9. How is my life a daily example of nonviolence?
   How does my community nurture peace and reconciliation within itself and in the wider world?

10. Do I live in harmony with all creation?
    Does my community exercise responsible stewardship?

11. How do I express love to those who are different from me?
    How does my community welcome those with whom we disagree?

12. When have I fallen short?
    When has my community avoided doing things that are hard?

Notes

Prologue

[1] Elizabeth Stirredge, *Strength in Weakness Manifest*, (London: J. Sowle, 1711), 19.

Introduction

[1] Gladys Kang'ahi, "Practical Discipleship," in Margery Post Abbott and Peggy Senger Parsons, eds., *Walk Worthy of Your Calling* (Richmond, IN: Friends United Press, 2004), 5.

[2] Elias Hicks, *Dear Friend: Letters & Essays of Elias Hicks*, ed. Paul Buckley (San Francisco: Inner Light Books, 2013), 53.

[3] Sarah Blackborow, *A Visit to the Spirit in Prison* (London: Thomas Simmons, 1658), 10–11.

[4] Joseph John Gurney, "Observations on the Distinguishing Views & Practices of the Society of Friends," in *Gurney's Works*, vol.1 (London: Charles Gilpin, Norwich: Joseph Fletcher, 1848), 76.

[5] George Fox, *Journal of George Fox*, ed. John Nickalls (London: Religious Society of Friends, 1975), 263.

[6] James Nayler, "A Discovery of the Wisdom which is from Beneath, And the Wisdom Which is from Above," in James Nayler, *Collection of Sundry Books, Epistles and Papers by James Nayler* (Cincinnati: B. C. Stanton, 1829), 108.

[7] William Allen, *Life of William Allen, with Selections from his Correspondence*, vol. 1 (Philadelphia: Henry Longstreth, 1847), 18.

Chapter 1

[1] Caroline Emelia Stephen, *Quaker Strongholds*, 3rd ed. (London: Edward Hicks, 1891), 10.

[2] Thomas Hamm, *The Transformation of American Quakerism: Orthodox Friends, 1800–1907* (Bloomington: Indiana University Press, 1992), 206n3.

[3] Margaret Fell, *Brief collection of remarkable passages and occurrences relating to Margaret Fell* (London: J. Sowle, 1710), 116.

Chapter 2

[1] William Penn, "Brief Account of the Rise and Progress of the People Called Quakers," in William Penn, *A Collection of the Works of William Penn*, vol. 1 (London: J. Sowle, 1726), 881.

[2] George Fox, *Journal of George Fox*, ed. John Nickalls (London: Religious Society of Friends, 1975), 11.

[3] Fox, *Journal of George Fox*, 98.

[4] Robert Barclay, "Apology for the True Christian Divinity," in *Truth Triumphant*, vol. 2 (New York: Benjamin C. Stanton, 1831), 357.

[5] This book is also available in a modern English version: Robert Barclay, *Barclay's Apology in Modern English*, ed. Dean Freiday (Newberg, OR: The Barclay Press, 1967).

[6] Anonymous, "To the Reader," in *A Collection of the Works of William Penn*, vol. 2 (London: J. Sowle, 1726), 2.

Notes

[7] William Penn, "Primitive Christianity Reviv'd," in Penn, *Works of William Penn*, 2:855.

[8] Penn, "Primitive Christianity Reviv'd," 853.

[9] John Burnyeat, John Watson, and William Penn, *Truth Exalted in the Writings of that Eminent and Faithful Servant of Christ John Burnyeat* (London: Thomas Northcott, 1691), 163.

[10] John Woolman, "Considerations on the True Harmony of Mankind, and How it is to be Maintained," in John Woolman, *Works of John Woolman*, vol. 2 (London: James Phillips, 1775), 30.

[11] James Nayler, "The Lamb's War against the Man of Sin," in Nayler, *Collection of Sundry Books*, 376.

[12] Penn, "People Called Quakers," 869.

[13] Anthony Benezet, *Serious Considerations on Several Important Subjects* (Philadelphia: Joseph Crukshank, 1778), 18.

[14] George Fox, "Epistle 169," in George Fox, *The Works of George Fox*, vol. 7 (Philadelphia: Marcus T. C. Gould; New York: Isaac T. Hopper, 1831), 157.

[15] Dorothy White, *A Call from God out of Egypt* (London, 1662), 5.

[16] Margaret Fell, *A Call unto the Seed of Israel* (London: Robert Wilson, 1668), 16–17.

Chapter 3

[1] Margaret Fell, "An Epistle to Convinced Friends," in *The life of Margaret Fox* (Philadelphia: Book Association of Friends, 1885), 88.

2. William Penn, "Primitive Christianity Reviv'd," in William Penn, *A Collection of the Works of William Penn*, vol. 2 (London: J. Sowle, 1726), 853.

3. George Fox, *Journal of George Fox*, ed. John L. Nickalls (London: Religious Society of Friends, 1975), 117.

4. Ann Docwra, *An Epistle of Love and Good Advice* (1683), 7.

5. George Fox, "Epistle 10," in *The Power of the Lord Is Over All*, ed. T. Canby Jones (Richmond, IN: Friends United Press, 1989), 7.

6. Job Scott, *The Knowledge of the Lord, the Only True God* (Philadelphia: Emmor Kimber, 1824), 9.

7. George Fox, "Epistle 227," in Fox, *The Power of the Lord Is Over All*, 185.

8. Fox, *Journal of George Fox*, 19.

9. Isaac Penington, "The Flesh and Blood of Christ in the Mystery, and in the Outward," in Isaac Penington, *The Works of Isaac Penington*, vol. 3 (Glenside, PA: Quaker Heritage Press, 1996), 367.

10. George Fox, "Journal or Historical Account of the Life, Travels, Sufferings of George Fox," in Fox, *The Works of George Fox*, vol. 2 (Philadelphia: Marcus T. C. Gould; New York: Isaac T. Hopper, 1831), 193.

11. Penn, "Primitive Christianity Reviv'd," 869.

12. George Fox, *Priests and Professors Catechisme* (London: Giles Calvert, 1657), 16.

13. Barclay, "Apology for the True Christian Divinity," 62, 67.

14. William Penn, "Some Fruits of Solitude," in Penn, *Works of William Penn*, 2:842.

Notes

[15] Isaac Penington, "Some Misrepresentations of Me concerning Church-Government," in Isaac Penington, *The Works of Isaac Penington*, vol. 4 (Glenside, PA: Quaker Heritage Press, 1996), 315.

[16] William Penn, "Brief Account of the Rise and Progress of the People Called Quakers," in Penn, *Works of William Penn*, 2: 869.

[17] John Woolman, *The Journal and Major Essays of John Woolman*, ed. Phillips P. Moulton (New York: Oxford University Press, 1971), 153–54.

[18] Philadelphia Yearly Meeting, *The Old Discipline* (Glenside, PA: Quaker Heritage Press, 1999), 25–26.

[19] Sarah Cheevers, as quoted in William Sewel, *The History of the Rise, Increase, and Progress, of the Christian People called Quakers* (Burlington, NJ: Isaac Collins, 1774), 350.

[20] Joseph Phipps, *Original and Present State of Man, Briefly Considered* (New York: William Ross, 1788), 62.

[21] Deborah Saunders, "Send Me," *Friends Journal* 44, no. 5 (May 1998): 15–16.

[22] Margaret Fell, *Declaration and Information from us the People of God called Quakers* (London: Thomas Simmons and Robert Wilson, 1660), 7.

[23] Fox, *Journal of George Fox*, 65.

[24] Louise Wilson, *Inner Tenderings* (Richmond, IN: Friends United Press, 1996), 173.

[25] Joseph Besse, *Collection of the Sufferings of the People Called Quakers* (London: Luke Hinde, 1753), 394.

Chapter 4

[1] Ann Branson, *Journal of Ann Branson* (Philadelphia: Wm. H. Pile's Sons, Printers, 1892), 374.

[2] Thomas Kelly, *A Testament of Devotion* (New York: Harper & Row, 1941), 121-22.

[3] Kelly, *A Testament of Devotion*, 110.

[4] Elizabeth Comstock, *Life and Letters of Elizabeth L. Comstock* (London: Headley Brothers, 1895), 256.

[5] Isaac Penington, "To Friends in Amersham," in Isaac Penington, *The Works of Isaac Penington*, vol. 2 (Glenside, PA: Quaker Heritage Press, 1996), 486.

[6] Gladys Kang'ahi, "Practical Discipleship," in Margery Post Abbott and Peggy Senger Parsons, eds., *Walk Worthy of Your Calling: Quakers and the Traveling Ministry* (Richmond, IN: Friends United Press, 2004), 3–4.

[7] Penn, "Brief Account of the Rise and Progress of the People Called Quakers," in *A Collection of the Works of William Penn*, vol. 1 (London: J. Sowle, 1726), 871.

[8] John Woolman, "On the Right Use of the Lord's Outward Gifts," in Woolman, *Works of John Woolman*, 2:18.

[9] Gardner, *Memoirs of the Life and Religious Labors of Sunderland P. Gardner*, 357.

[10] William Penn, "People Called Quakers," 877.

[11] Francis Howgill, "Francis Howgill's Testimony Concerning the Life, Death, Tryals, Travels, and Labours of Edward Burrough, That Worthy Prophet of the Lord," in Edward Burrough, *The Memorable Works of a Son of Thunder* (1672).

Notes

[12] Samuel Bownas, *Account of the Life, Travels, and Christian Experiences in the Work of the Ministry of Samuel Bownas* (London: James Phillips, 1795), 3.

[13] Peggy Senger Morrison, "Holy Boldness" (plenary address, Friends General Conference Gathering, St. Joseph, Minnesota, 2016). Peggy told me that she cannot take credit for this prayer. It was given to her by a Benedictine nun with instructions to repeat it as often as possible.

[14] Thomas Kelley, *A Testament of Devotion* (New York: Harper & Row, 1941), 92.

[15] Margaret Fell, "To Friends, Brethren, and Sisters, April 1700," in Elsa Glines, ed., *Undaunted Zeal: The Letters of Margaret Fell* (Richmond, IN: Friends United Press, 2003), 470.

[16] Anna Davis Hallowell, *James and Lucretia Mott: Life and Letters* (Boston: Houghton, Mifflin and Co.; Cambridge: The Riverside Press, 1884), 517.

[17] Hallowell, *James and Lucretia Mott*, 532.

[18] Hallowell, *James and Lucretia Mott*, 516.

[19] Robert Barrawe, "Robert Barrawe's Testimony concerning Sarah Beck," in Sarah Beck, *A Certain and True Relation of the Heavenly Enjoyments and Living Testimonies of God's Love unto Her Soul* (1680), 10.

Chapter 5

[1] John Punshon, "Some Reflections on Quakers and the Evangelical Spirit," in *Truth's Bright Embrace: Essays and Poems in Honor of Arthur O. Roberts*, ed. Paul N. Anderson and Howard R. Macy (Newberg, OR: George Fox University Press, 1996), 219. Available online at http://digitalcommons.georgefox.edu/truths_bright.

Also available from Inner Light Books

Primitive Christianity Revived
by William Penn
Translated into Modern English by Paul Buckley

    ISBN 978-0-9998332-0-9 (hardcover) $25
    ISBN 978-0-9998332-1-6 (paperback) $15

Jesus, Christ and Servant of God
Meditations on the Gospel According to John
By David Johnson

    ISBN 978-0-9970604-6-1 (hardcover) $35
    ISBN 978-0-9970604-7-8 (paperback) $25
    ISBN 978-0-9970604-8-5 (eBook) $12.50

The Anti-War
By Douglas Gwyn

    ISBN 978-0-9970604-3-0, (hardcover) $30
    ISBN 978-0-9970604-4-7, (paperback) $17.50
    ISBN 978-0-9970604-5-4, (eBook) $10

Our Life Is Love, the Quaker Spiritual Journey
By Marcelle Martin

    ISBN 978-0-9970604-0-9, (hardcover) $30
    ISBN 978-0-9970604-1-6, (paperback) $17.50
    ISBN 978-0-9970604-2-5, (eBook) $10

A Quaker Prayer Life
By David Johnson

    ISBN 978-0-9834980-5-6 (hardcover) $20
    ISBN 978-0-9834980-6-3 (paperback) $12.50
    ISBN 978-0-9834980-7-0 (eBook) $10

The Essential Elias Hicks
By Paul Buckley

    ISBN 978-0-9834980-8-7 (hardcover) $25
    ISBN 978-0-9834980-9-4 (paperback) $15

The Journal of Elias Hicks
Edited by Paul Buckley

> ISBN 978-0-9797110-4-6, (hardcover) $50
> ISBN 978-0-9797110-5-3, (paperback) $30

Dear Friend: The Letters and Essays of Elias Hicks
Edited by Paul Buckley

> ISBN 978-0-9834980-0-1 (hardcover) $45
> ISBN 978-0-9834980-1-8 (paperback) $25

The Early Quakers and 'the Kingdom of God'
By Gerard Guiton

> ISBN 978-0-9834980-2-5, (hardcover) $45
> ISBN 978-0-9834980-3-2, (paperback) $25
> ISBN 978-0-9834980-4-9, (eBook) $12.50

John Woolman and the Affairs of Truth
Edited by James Proud

> ISBN 978-0-9797110-6-0, (hardcover) $45
> ISBN 978-0-9797110-7-7, (paperback) $25

Cousin Ann's Stories for Children by Ann Preston
Edited by Richard Beards
Illustrated by Stevie French

> ISBN 978-0-9797110-8-4, (hardcover) $20
> ISBN 978-0-9797110-9-1, (paperback) $12

Counsel to the Christian-Traveller: also Meditations and Experiences
By William Shewen

> ISBN 978-0-9797110-0-8 (hardcover) $25
> ISBN 978-0-9797110-1-5 (paperback) $15

CPSIA information can be obtained
at www.ICGtesting.com
Printed in the USA
BVHW080951240321
603275BV00006B/614

9 780999 833230